Also by R
(Writing as S¹

More Than a Game
A story about football and other stuff

This groundbreaking, earthy novel for teen and young adult readers tells of how football (and the world) used to be. Sabina Park Rangers is the first team of black players to reach the final of the Watney's Challenge Cup. But coach Horace McIntosh has more selection problems than most because of arrests, a scam and an atmosphere of impending violence.

". . . Funny, poignant, illuminating.
The best football novel in years." – *Positive Magazine*

"I really enjoyed this book . . . It says so much about people . . . We need more writers like him . . . ." – Benjamin Zephaniah

What Goes Around

This much-acclaimed novel is a chilling insight into the minds of 'home-grown' terrorists. In the seedy, violent city where they live, former friends go their separate ways and become involved with two terrorist organizations. For Tyrone Swaby it is a matter of choice when he joins the 'Brothers of Islam' but for Robbie Walker it is his friendship with his old sparring partner Danny Maguire that gets him embroiled with an IRA operation taking place right on his doorstep.

". . . a story that grips you from the first page . . ." *UNTOLD* Magazine

". . . Young's is a deftly assured debut which provides British crime writing with a vibrant new voice." *The Times*

". . . A powerful and explosive novel . . ." *The Weekly Gleaner*

". . . *What Goes Around* is, to coin a cliché, a real page-turner. The mystery and intrigue just keeps on coming as the suspense builds to an explosive ending." *The Big Issues*

MEMOIRS OF
A KARATE FIGHTER

RALPH ROBB

Raldon Books

First published in 2006
by Raldon Books
Co. Cork
Ireland

A CIP catalogue record for this book is available from the
British Library

ISBN:0-9552169-2-3
ISBN-13:978-0-552169-2-3

Typeset by Dominic Carroll, Ardfield, Co. Cork
Cover design by Eric Dunne-Magner, Co. Cork
Front cover photograph by Ann de Haas, Ontario Canada
Printed and bound in the Republic of Ireland by BetaPrint Ltd., Dublin

Back-cover photograph is of the winning team at the
1977 United Kingdom Wado Ryu championships in London,
with K. Sakagami and P. Suzuki
More photographs are available at www.raldonbooks.com

This book is dedicated to the memory of Clinton Campbell

— Acknowledgements —

I owe a great debt of gratitude to the scores of young men who trained at the Wolverhampton YMCA karate club over the years. Their personalities and experiences have often inspired many of the characters and plots in my novels. Unfortunately, editorial and other constraints make it impossible to include the names of everyone, or the many, many anecdotes about their time at the YMCA. So as well as offering my thanks, I also extend my apologies to all those I have failed to mention.

— Foreword —

KARATE, AS PRACTISED in Japan, had its 'golden era' in the lead up to World War II. It was a period, when impelled by ultra-nationalist fervour, karateka trained to the very limits of human endurance. Many of Japan's young karate exponents never returned from the war but, of those who did survive, some went on to teach their art throughout America and Europe. The karate master Tatsuo Suzuki had been frustrated that he had been too young to enlist but twenty years after the war had ended he began establishing the style of Wado Ryu throughout Europe. Initially, the type of karate he taught was similar to the uncompromising sort in which he himself had been tutored. But karate had entered vastly different cultures and after initial calls in the British popular press for it to be banned, it was inevitable that the fighting art he had brought from Japan would alter as time went by.

The year in which I began my training was during British karate's heyday. In 1975, Britain defeated Japan in the final of the world championships in Long Beach, California and would go onto to dominate the world championships throughout the 1980s. While Britain was the foremost team in international karate competitions, a club called the Wolverhampton YMCA was, for a period, the top club in Britain. Therefore, by most objective reckoning, it was, during that time, one of the finest karate clubs in the world.

The YMCA club was, in many ways, a freak of nature, it was a series of coincidences which brought together outstanding fighters who just so happened to want to learn the art of karate at around the same place and at the same time. Their collective attitude could be summed up as: go anywhere, fight any style, under any rules – and use whatever referees you like. The team won so many tournaments that it would be impossible to record them all but amongst the YMCA's greatest achievements were two British All-styles titles, five national Wado Ryu championships and, in 1976, a national Shotokan championship – the only team, in the history of British karate, not to practise that style ever to do so. Hirokazu Kanazawa, arguably the greatest-ever Shotokan karateka, magnanimously led the applause as the YMCA triumphed over a team of his own students in the final. While watching the contest, Kanazawa sensei may have been reminded of the brutal fights that had taken place between rival schools while Japanese karate was in its infancy, as the 1976 *Shotokan Karate International* championships had been, by many people's reckoning, one of the bloodiest competitions to have ever taken place in Britain. A year later the tournament was made exclusive to Shotokan teams as the inter-style rivalry had led to so many injuries that it was considered unsafe to continue with its 'all-comers' criteria.

Within the YMCA's ranks were one world, three European and twelve national champions and it was my privilege to train with them. But their fights were not limited to what happened on the competition mat or within the dojo and many of the YMCA karate team were involved in situations of real ferocity out on some very mean streets, some of which I witnessed firsthand. My intention is not to glorify any action or person but to simply recount, to the best of my ability, the type of training and experiences I underwent to become a karate fighter.

The practise of martial arts is often characterized as a route to self-enlightenment and this book is a record of the path I walked as a much younger man and of the personalities, the triumphs, the adversities and the pitfalls that I encountered along the way.

Ralph Robb · June 2006

— Chapter One —

Under the sword lifted high
There is hell making you tremble;
But go ahead
And you have the land of bliss.
Miyamoto Musashi (1584 —1645)

THE BIG GUY had a knife. This was not a film shoot, nor a rehearsed demonstration, this was not a sporting competition – this was real, this was a matter of life and death. The man in front of him was a big guy too: Jerome Atkinson stood six-five and weighed two hundred and fifteen pounds of muscle – and unfortunately for the man with the knife he also had the innate fighting ability that one day would make him the all-styles karate heavyweight champion of the world.

There weren't too many people around who were physically bigger than Jerome but the man with a black tee-shirt stretched over his muscular chest was huge. I figured that he must have been from out of town because he was not the sort of man you could easily forget – and, judging by his behaviour, he obviously knew nothing of the reputation of the two men dressed in black suits and ties at the nightclub's door. The big stranger had ignored the queue and led his gang to the entrance. He claimed to be a relative of the owner but my cousin Ewart Campbell had told him and his gang to get to the back of the line. Ewart was nowhere near as big

1

but at a little more than six feet, his lean frame reminded me of the world champion boxer and kayo specialist Tommy Hearns, but perhaps he carried even more explosive power in his fists. One of the group shouted that no man could treat them so disrespectfully and live. People in the queue immediately began to shuffle back, some tripping over in their attempts to get out of harm's way. Angry shouts echoed amid the thudding bass that filtered out from the dance floor and into the balmy night air. A young woman screamed as she saw a blade being drawn.

I watched from the foyer and like the rest of the onlookers, I was excited and fearful all at once. But no one was looking at me; I was not a player in this unfolding drama but just a kid of seventeen who was out for a good time with a couple of friends. Panic put more of the crowd spilling out onto the road but the chance to see a genuine street fight kept them hovering; like the crowds who had once flocked to the gladiatorial contests in ancient Rome, they were drawn by the spectacle of violence and the scent of danger. I may have been inexperienced but I felt compelled to step forward and help out my two fellow karateka: as formidable as they were, a ratio of six to two did not seem fair odds. Again, no one seemed to notice me as I sidled up to Jerome and Ewart.

The sight of the blade that had caused the woman's scream had me transfixed until a flurry of activity drew my gaze away. One of the gang had thrown a punch at Ewart, a British light-heavyweight all-styles champion, and had rapidly paid for his rash action when he hit the ground with a sickening thud. Another of the gang brushed past me to intervene and without any conscious thought, my arm went across his throat. He struggled and lashed out. Now oblivious to the melee going on around me, I managed to put him into a choke hold. He was unconscious within seconds and I lowered him to the ground – just in time to see the man with the knife standing in the middle of the street ranting and spitting threats while moving toward Jerome. Jerome took two languid steps forward. It was a response the knife man had not expected. By this time five men were on the ground and the crowd had spread across the street in a large arc and I sensed that a good proportion of them were still silently baying for more blood. I was concerned for Jerome's well-being but like the rest of the onlookers I was curious too. This, after all, was what we trained for, this was the life-or-death situation we were told to imagine while punishing our bodies in the dojo. This would be a moment of truth.

The big guy was yelling again as he made his move. With astonishing speed Jerome moved forward to meet his attacker and then, with perfect timing, he sidestepped and the knife went past him. I recognized his movement as a variation of a basic technique I had been taught in the dojo. The Japanese call it *irimi* (entering) and when combined with *kawashi* (avoiding) the result can be devastating as the attacker's own momentum is used against him. I heard a grunt and the sound of the blade dropping onto the road as Jerome's open hand hit the big man's throat just below his Adam's apple. The man straightened and then a fist crashed against his jaw. The crack brought a gasp from the onlookers and two large hands spread over a disbelieving face, moments after blood and teeth had sprayed from the big man's mouth. His legs folded, as if he were about to sit on an invisible stool, before an instinct for survival straightened them again. He swivelled and staggered down the road like a drunk with another three groggy men following him, one of them falling down twice as he went. The man at my feet coughed and slowly stood up. He swayed and scratched his head as he tried to figure out what had gone on. He did not even look at me but the sights of Jerome and Ewart and his fleeing comrades were enough for him to take off after them.

My initial apprehension had been instantly turned into exhilaration. There was a clarity to the technique Jerome had used that had previously eluded me. I promised myself then that I'd practise this move over and over again in the dojo. This was the first time I had seen it executed with such brutal perfection. I said as much to Jerome. He smiled down at me and shook his head as he told me it had been far from perfection because his foot had slipped slightly as he threw the punch, otherwise it would have knocked

the big man unconscious. Ewart was pumped up and said to
Jerome that he should not have let the big guy get away but should
have run after him and finished him off. He pointed at the man
who had taken the first swing; he was still lying awkwardly against
the concrete steps. If it were not for a trickle of blood from the
man's ears, I would have thought he was sleeping peacefully. Ewart
was deadly serious when he said that anyone who drew a knife on
him would be waking up in a hospital ward. The fight did sum up
the men's differing attitudes: Jerome had been content to disarm
the man but Ewart would have only been satisfied with the knife
man stretched out in the road. Part of me wanted to say that *I* had
rendered one man unconscious but neither Jerome nor Ewart
seemed to be aware of my contribution and as I looked across the
street to the police station I thought it would be for the best if I
said nothing about it. Two policemen had witnessed the whole
event and were laughing to themselves. They looked across to the
man who had yet to regain consciousness and applauded – I
thought sarcastically – and I feared that they might be waiting for
backup before coming over to arrest the three of us. I was back to
being apprehensive again: how would I explain my arrest to my
parents who did not even know that I was going to a nightclub?

After an ambulance had taken away the man on the steps, I had
wanted to leave but felt duty-bound to stay in case there was more
trouble. I was also convinced that if the police did not turn up,
then the big guy would be back with reinforcements. Jerome and
Ewart carried on as if completely unconcerned. Either they were
very good actors, or they genuinely didn't share any of my worries.
As it turned out, they had correctly reckoned that the troublemakers would be spending at least one night in a hospital's
Accident and Emergency department and one big man would
be having his broken jaw fixed with wires.

It had not been the first time I had seen a knife used in a fight
nor would it be the last. I grew up in an area of town where there
were a lot of fights; it was a place where a large number of immigrants from the Carribean and the Indian subcontinent had settled

4

and there was often trouble between them and the local white youths. My parents had arrived from Jamaica three years before I was born and I was followed into the world by three sisters. Consequently, most of my leisure time was spent in the company of my male cousins and friends. Violence, or the threat of violence, were constant companions as I made my way along the streets to meet up with the rest of the gang. As a child of no more than twelve years old I had witnessed brawls between kids of my own age that were fought with serious and violent intent. One vivid childhood memory was of my young cousin Trevor smashing a bottle during a fight with the intention of pushing it into the face of another kid who, only two minutes before, had been his best friend. But that was an extreme episode and usually violence amongst the local youngsters was more low-key and came about as arguments turned into fights over trivial matters, such as a foul while playing soccer, or the alleged theft of a sweet.

But there were also more serious threats in the town in which I lived: it was common back in the 1970s for a black man or boy to find himself being chased by groups of white men wielding sticks or knives for simply having the nerve to walk along a street in a particular area. Many of my friends and relatives had experienced that sort of frightening encounter and as a result there were parts of town that my friends and I refused to visit. But this attitude was by no means exceptional, nor simply down to race or colour: for young men it was often about gangs and territory.

The nuclei of our little gang were my cousins Clinton, Errol and Trevor, our friend Leslie and me. Whether or not it was simply the hostile atmosphere about the town that turned us into fighters I am still not sure. Clinton and Errol had older brothers whose greater experience of the world had led them to conclude that we had to toughen up. Part of this 'toughening up' process involved arranging fights for me with other boys at the local park. Ewart and Kingsley let it be known that they had placed money on the result and did not expect me to lose. Frequently, they would give me a taste of what to expect from them if I did. Once, when I refused to fight, they staked me out in the park and let me bake for hours under a blazing sun. Such were their reputations, no one dared to rescue me. It was a tactic they had picked up from some western movie in which Jimmy Stewart, or perhaps John Wayne, had been similarly tethered in a baking desert by Apache warriors.

Outside of real fights, the gang's free time was occupied with the fantasy fighting of kung fu movies. Errol, Clinton and I spent our Friday and Saturday nights at the Colosseum cinema where the audience would be 99% male and 100% black and boisterous. Kung fu movies were all the craze when we were teenagers and the rat-infested cinema was always packed for its late-night weekend shows. The atmosphere in the Colosseum was always very different to what I would find at the cinemas in the town centre, as there were always plenty of people in the audiences who were willing to supply a running commentary on the action.

Of all the kung fu stars, Wang Yu was the favourite at the Colosseum. But why kung fu movies and why Wang? For black guys of my age the badly scripted, poorly dubbed Cantonese films were a cheap escape from the grind of daily life; their carefully choreographed fight scenes acted as a release for people who were otherwise preoccupied with thoughts of real violence. It was easy to fantasize about thrashing either the cops who hassled us, or the thugs who attacked us, as simply as Wang dispatched his foes. As for Wang Yu himself, his popularity was, in part, due to his name: it had not been corrupted with a 'Bruce' or a 'Jackie' – from which we surmised that he had not 'sold out', which back then was a significant phrase for young black people. But this turned out not to be strictly true and as Wang's popularity grew his name became 'Jimmy' Wang Yu. But this uncomfortable truth was not allowed to get in the way of unalloyed hero-worship. Also, his fighting style was admired as it was more traditional than Lee's and less clowning than Chan's. And lastly, in his films there were only Chinese people and so we were transported to another world in which the hero wasn't always a white man and it was the Japanese, rather than black men, who were the stereotypical bad guys.

One Friday night, shortly after we had left the Colosseum, Clinton, Errol and I had been chased by a gang of white men armed with clubs. Probably frustrated that they could not find an unaccompanied victim, they had decided to stop their car and chase three teenage boys. We scattered and I ducked into an alley that led into back streets and rear gardens. The men must have sensed easy prey and followed me into the dark. I couldn't understand it, I was a good athlete but my legs refused to respond, it was as if I were running in a tank of treacle. Breathing hard, I rounded another corner – and something hit me. The impact was severe, arms and legs violently clashed as our bodies collapsed onto the hard ground. Fearing imminent death, I screamed out loud.

"Shut up," croaked a familiar voice, "this way." It was Clinton: he had returned to help me.

After a short distance we had to scale a high wire-mesh fence. Within moments the men were on the other side furiously growling obscenities and shaking the mesh but we all knew that there was no way they were going to get over the fence. As they continued to hurl their threats, I wanted to get away but Clinton stood his ground with an air of contemptuous indifference. I stared on in disbelief as he opened his flies and began pissing through the mesh. Almost hysterical with rage, the men jumped back, as if Clinton's urine was a deadly acid.

On trembling legs, I ran back to the cinema with Clinton hoping to see Errol and to look for the safety of a crowd. "So, Ralph," he said to me, as we slowed down to walking pace, "are you going to start training with the rest of us?"

At first I was too angry, or too scared, to speak. My lungs were still burning and my legs remained shaking as adrenalin continued to course through them. I paused before responding. The training he referred to was in karate at the local YMCA. At first I had been dismissive when Clinton and Leslie started training: I was supposed to be the tough guy of our little group, the one who took part in bare knuckle fights in order to win money for

Clinton's older brothers, and I had already told him that I did not need this martial arts stuff. But in truth I was wary of getting involved. The YMCA karate club had a fearsome reputation, and I had heard tales, recounted in the most reverential tones, about the instructor who had once beaten up a gang of Hell's Angels and had knocked out a genuine Chinese kung fu master; about the tough men – including Clinton's older brothers – who trained there; about injuries; about journeys to the hospital; about guys who thought they could handle themselves but who had quit after just one session. "No," I had previously told Clinton, "I'll stick to my athletics." But now such a response seemed pathetic because I knew that behind Clinton's question was the idea that we should have stood and fought, that we should have levelled the club-wielding white guys in a fashion similar to that of Wang Yu's.

A week later I enrolled at one of Britain's toughest and most successful karate clubs. In retrospect I am now keenly aware of just how much that decision changed my life, because it was not until I left school and entered the adult world, did I fully appreciate just how perilous the place in which I grew up could be.

— Chapter Two —

There is timing in everything. Timing cannot be mastered without a great amount of practise.
Miyamoto Musashi — The Ground Book

"ICHI . . . NI . . . SAN . . . SHI . . ." The sensei's calls were rhythmic and hypnotic. For more than two very intense hours we had punched and kicked up and down the length of the dojo. It was an exercise that was punctuated with exchanges of techniques with a partner before we returned to our lines and started all over again. "Ichi . . . Ni . . . San . . . Shi . . ."

The instructor who was putting us through all this agony was Eddie Cox. He was a broad figure whose demeanour gave him a presence that made him seem far more powerful than anyone else in the dojo. Years before, when I had first joined the club, the first thing I had noticed about him was the thickness of his hands. Protruding from the sleeves of his heavy canvas gi, they resembled great lumps of black iron that had been forged in one of the local foundries for only one purpose: to inflict pain. With his dark skin and broad features he looked like a sawn-off version of a young George Foreman — only something in his eyes made him look a lot meaner. The rumours about his toughness that I had heard while I was still a schoolkid had not done him justice. But it was not just karate that had hardened him. He had once been the toughest kid in the toughest school in town before he

9

had ever started training. Until the day it was closed down, St. Joseph's had a reputation for turning out more criminals than academics and was nicknamed 'Joey's Jailhouse'. Most of the boys attending the Catholic secondary school were of Italian or Irish backgrounds and Eddie was one of only a handful of black pupils – and it was an experience that had left its mark. In an institution in which you were either predator or prey, Eddie decided it was better to become the king of that particular jungle. The tales about the severity of the training sessions he ran had been no exaggerations either. There had been many occasions when I had cursed my cousin Clinton for talking me into accompanying him to the YMCA, mostly as I was helped from the dojo nursing a pulled muscle, a sore abdomen, or a bruised face.

After more than five years of dedicated training, Clinton and I were brown belts and it felt as though we had become members of a larger family unit. A few of us within this extended family were on the fringes of promotion that would put us on par with some of the black belts. Still in our late teens, we were so cocksure of ourselves that we brashly thought that, on a physical level, we were already as good as the dan grades. The harsh training regime had made our bodies strong and hard but our youthful limbs kept us flexible and fast. In order to rearrange the established 'food chain' to more in keeping with our own inflated self-image, there would have to be confrontation. I would have done well to remember one of my mother's favourite adages: *Be careful what you wish for, you might just get it!*

The style of karate practised at the YMCA was Wado Ryu, which, according to modern translations, means 'way of peace school'. Wado was created by a Japanese jujitsu master named Hironori Ohtsuka who blended the art he had studied from the age of six with the Okinawan fighting system that only became universally known as 'karate' in the 1930s. When Master Ohtsuka visited the Wado Ryu United Kingdom national championships in 1975, the first year the YMCA had entered the tournament, he had commented to other Japanese instructors that out of all the karateka who were competing, it was Eddie Cox's team who had captured "the true essence of Wado." This was high praise indeed, and had probably been accorded by the kancho (the head of the style) because of the attitude of the YMCA fighters. Whatever else about philosophy or tradition, it was during the period when Japan was making military forays into China and Manchuria, that Ohtuska developed his style of karate. First and foremost, it was designed to be a potent combat system. Like many other Japanese budo masters of that time, Ohtsuka had been recruited into the ultra-nationalist and secret Black Dragon Society, the members of which had carried out spying missions and assassinations for their government in Chinese and Russian territories. Collectively, their minds were set on refining ancient methods of killing and Ohtsuka unashamedly appropriated techniques from other styles of martial arts if they were shown to be effective. But like his good friend Morihei Ueshiba, the founder of modern aikido, Ohtsuka knew that without the proper attitude – as he had witnessed within the YMCA team that day – all the good techniques in the world counted for little in a real combat situation unless they were performed with 'fighting spirit'.

After training for a decade with Gichin Funakoshi, the man credited with bringing karate to Japan from Okinawa, Ohtsuka became frustrated with his sensei's stricture that forbade his students to spar with each other, as at the time it was deemed that karate was far too dangerous. However, this did not sit well with Hironori Ohtsuka; he had been training in bushido (the way of the warrior) since he was a child and knew that without the element of sparring, any combat system would be limited in its effectiveness. Initially, he and other like-minded students donned kendo armour breastplates and held secret sparring sessions. Then he did something that, to this day, remains unforgivable to some Japanese Shotokan karateka: he broke away and formed his own school. It was a move that was implicitly critical of Funakoshi's philosophy and methods. Not only that, following the suggestion of his friend and colleague Eiichi Eriguchi, he called his school

Wado, which while nowadays can be benevolently interpreted as 'way of peace', in 1934, when patriotic fanaticism was sweeping through Japan, it seems more likely that, given Ohtsuka's membership of the Black Dragon Society, Wado would have been more correctly translated as 'Japanese way' – which again could be construed as a slight to the Okinawan-born Funakoshi.

But whatever about Ohtuska's original motivations, it seemed that Eddie Cox and the rest of the black belts had interpreted the Wado ethos as: there is nothing as peaceful as a man who is laid out unconscious. In the time I had spent training at the YMCA, more than a few boxers and practitioners of other martial arts had been drawn to the dojo by its reputation – in order to test themselves as well as the members of the karate club – and I had seen this ethos put into practice with frightening efficiency.

Always prepared to enter any sort of karate competition, the original YMCA team were pioneers who travelled the length and breadth of Britain during the 1970s, when – fuelled by the sort of films I had watched at the Colosseum and by the *Kung Fu* television series – participation in the martial arts had reached unprecedented levels. For many young black men of that era, carrying a knife as a means of self-defence, or participation in an oriental fighting art seemed almost obligatory.

In keeping with the way Eddie Cox had been taught at the Temple Karate Club in Birmingham by his Japanese instructors, Toru Takamizawa and Peter Suzuki, I was introduced to jiyu kumite (free-fighting) very quickly. The more senior members would take it easy with me by giving me openings on which to capitalise; they rarely attacked and when they did their techniques were light and relatively slow. To some it may have seemed that they were toying with their prey but I took it as their way of helping me to develop correct techniques and self-confidence.

The days of such easy lessons soon went and, as I became more proficient, every little advance in my technique was paid for with the pain of constant repetition and, on the occasions when I failed to concentrate, with blood and humiliation.

"Ichi . . . ni . . . san . . . shi . .," Cox sensei continued to call out. Sweat ran into my eyes and down my back. Those of us on the second row did our best to match the black belts at the front for speed and power. I could see vapours of perspiration rise from them and the fuggy taste of sweat coated my tongue as I took in gulps of air. Our white karate suits clung to our skin as we did our best to focus our minds, while silently wishing that our agonies would come to a halt after the next technique. "More snap!" urged the sensei, "just ten more." No one believed him, after that there would be a call for a "last five". The blood in my gums started to boil, my muscles felt knotted and spent. With a last determined effort my techniques became venomous, now I was imagining punching the instructor, the black belts in front of me, the person who had scratched my car, or anyone else who had upset me that day. "Good," said the sensei, "last ten!"

Ten? It was never a last ten! To a man we were outraged. Without any instruction to do so, we started to shout with every punch and kick. Disregarding the signals from our sinews that silently begged for mercy, we dredged up the strength to move with renewed vigour. For a few moments nothing else existed other than the challenge to get to the end of the session without collapsing.

The concrete floor had become slippery and the vapour on the cold glass condensed and formed little rivulets that ran along the rusted metal frames. The misty windows not only indicated the intensity of our efforts but they also shielded us from what was happening in the world outside and, more immediately, the distracting activities of the prostitutes who peddled their wares on the street corner. I often wondered what someone peering in at us would make of the scene. To those who never had the dubious pleasure of putting on a karate uniform, or *gi* as it is called in Japanese, it might have appeared that we were engaged in some sort of bizarre ritual or an elaborate dance as we reacted in unison to our partners' movements. It was a dance designed to expose the weaknesses of a partner, a dance that was periodically punctuated with a violent exchange of punches, kicks, strikes and throws amid a cacophony of loud shouts – kiais – that echoed around the hall's cold whitewashed walls.

Finally, our efforts were brought to a halt with a shout of "*Yame!*" The sensei then sent those of us who were not black belts to kneel at the margins of the concrete floor. We would have to anxiously wait for our turn. I exchanged a nervous smile with Clinton. Leslie looked untroubled, he knew his diminutive size (he had stopped growing at five-foot-four) would probably protect him from what lay ahead for some of us. The tiredness of my limbs tempted me to sprawl out onto the floor, which was ominously painted blood-red, but it was a temptation I quickly dispelled; such a course of action would certainly have led to some sort of painful reminder of correct dojo etiquette. Fifty press-ups on the knuckles were a favourite punishment.

We watched the six black belts perform a series of crisply executed techniques. I did not know how they were doing it, but their high-velocity punches snapped, their fast kicks cracked, as sinewy limbs cut through the air. They shared a lot in common with each other: they had been awarded their dan grades by Japanese masters; they were in their mid-twenties and at the peak of their powers; and, with the exception of Declan Byrne, they were black men who had been born in Jamaica. They were the first team, the elite, and although some of us who were kneeling had recently won the Chester and North Wales Open and the Northwest of England Open championships, to be rated only good enough to make it into the second team made our triumphs of little consolation. Clinton and I longed to be in the first team and by our reckoning, given there were five fighters and two reserves in a karate team, there was at least one place up for grabs.

The YMCA had established itself as the top Wado Ryu club in Britain during the previous five years and in recognition of this Eddie Cox had been appointed as national Wado team coach, although a Japanese instructor continued to hold a nominal post. And while the YMCA had triumphed at almost every other 'open' competition, winning the newly-inaugurated British Karate

Federation Clubs' championship would make its status as the country's top club official. The tournament was fast approaching and the YMCA would be entering two teams but, along with Clinton, I no longer wanted to be in the 'B' team. It would be only a matter of time, maybe only minutes, before we would get our opportunity. There were thirty other students to choose from but if Clinton and I were called to fight one of the black belts, we would know that we were being considered for a first team place.

"*Yame!*" the sensei shouted again.

The black belts immediately ceased their actions. All eyes followed Eddie Cox. He began to talk of the fighting techniques that had just been so expertly demonstrated and of the upcoming tournament. But his words were indistinct to me: I was so tired that all I could do was to listen for any mention of my name. The sensei began to pace in front of us and pointed to those he wanted to pair off with the five black belts who had remained in a line. Three were already on their feet before he pointed to Clinton and me.

I respected them – but I had no fear of any of the black belts. I was apprehensive about which one of them I would be matched with but only because of how it might affect my chances of selection for the first team. All the black belts had a different style of fighting that in some way reflected their personalities and every one of them had won some sort of a national title. Eddie Cox and Declan Byrne had the most traditional outlook on karate training. The two men were very similar in many ways, despite one being a black Jamaican and the other a white Irishman: both men had very good karate techniques and a vicious streak that lay well hidden under gregarious personas until they donned a karate gi or were faced with a real life combat situation. Although their approach did not best suit competition karate (as both were of the opinion that sport was something to be played and karate was something that had to be lived) they had both won British titles at junior level and were members of the original team that had won so many tournaments. Declan and Eddie had worked side by side as electricians and had on occasions been compelled to use

15

their martial arts skills while working on building sites. Men who had heard of Eddie Cox's reputation – and thought little of it – sometimes challenged him to a fight. On occasions they were told if they could get past Declan (and they never did) he would fight them, but if he and Declan were pressed for time and had work to do, Eddie would knock them out if they persisted with their challenges. As well as working together they were as of one mind when it came to karate. They attended seminars that were organized by Tatsuo Suzuki and the other Japanese instructors and when the time came for Eddie to take his third dan examination, it was Declan who had accompanied him for the week-long course in London. The club's two outstanding competitors were Ewart Campbell and Jerome Atkinson. Both Ewart and Jerome competed at international level and had the exceptional confidence found in real top class fighters. Just below them as competitors were Chester Morrison, who was an all-styles lightweight national champion, and the much broader Hugo Robinson, who had won a national Wado Ryu title.

We lined up in front of the black belts and I found myself facing Chester Morrison. I was momentarily happy that I was not facing either Ewart or Jerome. Chester tended to treat sparring as an exercise and kept his punches light, unlike Hugo Robinson, a bear of a man whose front hand punch would leave indentations in the flesh of his opponents; and most definitely unlike Eddie Cox, or Declan Byrne, who were unpredictable and sometimes treated sparring in the dojo like a brawl in an alleyway, or the fights they'd had on building sites.

Eddie Cox inspected the two lines. "No, no," he said, "Clinton, you go with Chester. Ralph, pair up with Jerome." I suppose it made sense. Clinton was closer to Chester's weight than I. But although I had grown close to six-feet and weighed around 190 pounds I was a midget compared to Jerome. We bowed with the command of "*Rei*": the coloured belts bending from the waist whilst the black belts responded with a curt nod of the head. This was followed with a shout of "*Hajime!*" and the sparring erupted all around me.

With an opponent of my own size and ability I sometimes took chances in order to draw him out. My tactics would vary depending on the adversary: I could fall back into a defensive mode and give him a false sense of security; or I could be aggressive and attempt to intimidate him by throwing fast and hard combinations of punches. These were the same combinations I practised with Clinton in my backyard, or with my friend Mick at the factory, the same punches I threw at an always-compliant reflection in my bedroom mirror.

Against Jerome, no such options were available to me. He was the dominant one. I tried to attack but whatever I threw at him was returned with interest. It was not long before my attacks were halted by hurtful counter punches to my body. I thought briefly about Declan Byrne who trained with Jerome a daily basis: while I had a growing admiration for his ability to absorb punishment I did begin to have suspicions about his sanity. When he was not taking blows from Jerome, he would spend his leisure time smashing his fists against a wooden post called a makiwara that he had erected in his backyard, when (in his words) there wasn't much on TV.

I tried another attack on Jerome but the techniques that had worked time and again in my bedroom mirror failed me when I needed them most. My composure was being eroded, punch by punch, block by block. All thoughts of strategy had vanished: it had become a fight for me to save face. I launched another attack in an attempt to stop the onslaught but Jerome's fist thudded onto my body and my own punches fell short. I told myself to cool down, to wait for him to attack, and then hit him with a counterpunch as soon as he moved forward. I looked into his eyes for an indication of his next move but they remained expressionless. Suddenly, he shifted his stance to attack; I moved to counter him and instantly realized that his manoeuvre was merely a feint. I was already committed and I had no choice but to follow through with my punch. I saw his rear leg leave the ground but my block was little more than a futile gesture. I braced myself for the impact an

17

instant before I heard the sickening thud – or was it more of a crack? For a second or two I remained transfixed, too frightened to move. I heard the students kneeling behind me sucking in air as they waited for my reaction. It was as though I had become an alabaster figure and they were expecting me to shatter into a thousand tiny pieces. The next thing I heard was the sensei shouting for the sparring to halt. I also heard the concern in his voice. Jerome took hold of my shoulders and asked if I were okay. I nodded. It was difficult to speak but I was grateful that his concerned grip had stopped me sagging to the floor. Sensei approached and took a long look as I managed to tell him that I was only winded.

Satisfied that there was no more for us to give, the session was called to a close. The coloured belts were told to rise for the final bow and I was glad that I had managed to save some face by not collapsing onto the concrete floor as they had expected. As we made our way to the changing room, Clinton came over to me. He looked me over for a second and rested a hand on my shoulder. "Hey, Ralph," he laughed, "that was one bitch of a kick, man."

I responded with a wince. The road to the first team was going to be a hard and painful one to travel.

— Chapter Three —

Today is victory over yourself of yesterday;
tomorrow is your victory over lesser men.
Miyamoto Musashi — The Water Book

THE EARLY MORNING routine within the factory where I
worked had not changed since my first day there. Harold, as
always, arrived before anyone else, at least three-quarters of an
hour before the buzzer that would sound for the shift to begin.
After opening up the maintenance department he proceeded to
make the tea in a huge, unwashed enamel teapot. It was hardly
a ceremony but Harold had his own peculiar way of doing things
and to give the pot's encrusted brown interior anything but the
briefest of swills in cold water was something approaching sacri-
lege. Editions of tabloid newspapers, the most intellectual reading
matter in the canteen, lay waiting on the long table while faded
pinups from the older editions adorned the unpainted cement
block walls.

I had not had a decent sleep in the two days since my bout with
Jerome. The pain in my chest was worse at nights as the darkness
served only to amplify the pain. In desperation, I found lying
on my back on my hard bedroom floor did offer a modicum of
relief. Breathing was the main problem because my chest could
not expand without causing intense pain.

Mick Davies, a fellow maintenance fitter, could see that I was not my usual self. When I told him that I would not be turning up for our fifteen-minute training session during break time he asked what was wrong. I told him that I had a bit of a muscle strain, rather than my chest was feeling so tender that if he so much as touched me, he would, for the first time, see me howling in agony. He voiced his disappointment and playfully punched me on the arm. The tiny shockwaves travelled to the centre of my chest and had me grinding my teeth but I somehow managed not to show my discomfort until he had headed off to the canteen.

Mick was a few years older than I was but he had uncontrollable mousey-coloured hair and a cherub face that made him look more like a schoolkid. He was also well known around the factory for his prowess as a Shotokan karate black belt. When we had first met, I refrained from letting on that I also studied karate but as we got better acquainted, I confessed that I was a fellow exponent. Initially, my revelation was met with a hint of condescension when I mentioned the colour of the belt I wore but that quickly changed to almost overwhelming admiration when I told him that I trained at the YMCA.

It did not take long for our working relationship to turn into a friendship. Mick was born, bred and still lived in an area that had a completely different ethnic make-up to the one in which I had been brought up. He once commented to others that I was the first black person with whom he'd had a proper conversation. At first I couldn't make out whether this was an expression of either his guilt or pride. But, as I learnt, with Mick it was a simple expression of fact. My first interaction with him happened during my second day as a fresh-faced apprentice when he had ordered me and another new recruit to go to an isolated area of the factory. As we entered the large assembly room and made our way to report to the foreman, I sensed something was wrong. A group of hard-looking women began slowly encircling us, but a well-honed instinct for survival had me turning and running for the fire exit. I was only just through the doors when I heard the screams of the other apprentice. I later learned they had stripped him of his garments and rubbed black grease over his private parts. I found Mick almost crying with laughter but when he saw my terror he doubled over and his face turned so crimson that he looked in dire need of oxygen. I was not sure how to react but as I had escaped, I found it easy to forgive him for sending me for the apprentices' initiation rite.

I had thought about telling Mick about my injury but macho pride prevented me from doing so. Such was the reputation of the YMCA that to admit to pain seemed like an act of betrayal. Pain was something we had trained to accept from the first day: the sort that was self-inflicted in order to push us to the very limits of endurance; and the type inflicted by others so as to ensure that in a fight we did not immediately collapse nor surrender. But as the day wore on, I felt the urgent need to share my pain with someone. When it finally became too much to bear, I pretended that I was going to the toilet but I made a diversion to the first aid room when I thought no one was looking.

The factory nurse was Brenda, a short woman who was almost as wide as she was tall. Her face was as pleasant as her disposition but there were times as she saw me approach, when her demeanour became that of an old fashioned, no-nonsense matron.

"You again, Mr. Robb, what is it now?" she asked.

"The same as last time," I replied, "I keep hurting myself just so I can see you, Brenda."

Her stern face softened. "You are going to get me talked about. I see more of you than any other person in this factory," she chuckled. Then changing back to a more serious tone, she asked me the real reason for my visit.

"It's my chest," I replied. "I've taken a knock and now I can't breathe properly."

"Let me guess. You've been playing kung fu games again. When will you ever learn?" she said scornfully, before ordering me to take off my shirt and lie on the bed.

She began by examining my ribs. Her touch was gentle and despite my discomfort I smiled at her. Clearing her throat, she said, "Can't seem to find anything wrong so far."

Then, placing one hand on top of the other, she gently pressed down on my chest. It was if an electric current had shot through my entire body. My arms and legs stiffened as I let out a loud groan from between my clenched teeth.

She frowned and then said, "This is worse than I first thought. I think you've got a cracked sternum. I'm not equipped, nor am I qualified to treat it."

My first thought was of missing training and the British Clubs' championships. "Can't you just bandage it up for me?" I asked.

"I'll tell you what I'll do. I'll put on a couple of bandages for you, but you must promise to go and see your doctor today."

"I promise, Brenda."

She rummaged through her medicine cabinet and then placed two tablets onto my palm. "Take these for the pain. They act quite quickly," she said.

"I'd rather take the pain. I don't like taking pills unless I really have to."

She shook her head, as though unimpressed with my show of youthful machismo. "It's your choice," she sighed and then with a hint of a menace she added, "but I think I should warn you that I'm about to make you scream."

As she unwrapped the rolls of bandages, I studied her expression. She pursed her lips in a way I imagined a person would do when contemplating doing something unpleasant to another living being. I then looked to the tablets in my hand and said, "Can I have a glass of water with these, please?"

*

It had been a long and frustrating day at the factory. Several key breakdowns had meant that I had to work overtime but at least the pills that Brenda had given me had taken the edge off the pain. It was late in the evening as I drove for home. My route did not take me far from the dojo and the closer I got to the club, the stronger was the temptation for me to abandon my plans of going to my doctor's surgery. If Brenda was correct about my sternum being cracked – and I thought she was – I couldn't see the point in seeing a doctor. I supposed he would tell me that there wasn't much he could do for me but to tell me to rest. My priority was to make it into the team and such was my motivation that I had actually considered training that evening but fate had conspired for me to be late. So I figured, reluctantly, that some greater power was telling me to take the evening off.

After removing my shoes I entered the dojo. The damp, sweaty smell of endeavour hung heavy in the air. Following *dojo kun,* or etiquette, I made a bow and then, trying to remain as discrete as possible, I stood at the edge of the floor.

For several minutes it seemed as though my presence had gone unnoticed until the sensei approached me. He said, "Mr Robb, if you can't be bothered to train for such an important competition please wait outside." I could tell that he was angered by what he thought was my indiscipline until he saw the pained expression on my face. Perhaps it reminded him of the heavy kick I had taken the previous session. "Never mind," he added, nodding at a solitary chair, "just sit down and watch, you might learn something."

Even though I knew I had a legitimate reason for missing training, there were those who were close by who could not resist whispering taunts about me thinking of myself as too good to practise. From a black belt I would have accepted it as a gentle reprimand but from a fellow, or lesser, grade I considered such a remark as an attack on my dedication. Rivalry, and simple naked ambition, were behind the snide comments; after all, competition for places in the team was not only fierce but it was also encouraged and often some students would use whatever means they could to score a psychological point.

But it was not long before I became engrossed in what was happening in the dojo. While training, I had only time to concentrate on my own technique and that of whomever I was facing as we went through a series training drills. The YMCA placed a particular emphasis on working in pairs and Eddie Cox had put us training in that manner from the first lesson. Techniques executed up and down the hall or in a kata were not undervalued but it was the pair-work which taught the sense of distance, or *maai*, and what it is to receive as well as deliver a technique. I watched the training grow in intensity and saw how we were also being taught a mastery over fear. Lower-ranking students had paired off with the senior grades and faced spiteful kicks that whipped through the air and punches that snapped and cracked. But it wasn't only the higher grades who were executing techniques with such proficiency. Clinton was having a difficult time with a karateka who was a couple of grades lower than him: a purple belt nicknamed Trog. I was surprised, as up until that point I thought that Clinton had never looked better; his poise, balance and sheer speed had made him an excellent fighter but now he was being caught with blows from a much bulkier and less talented karateka. As the session went on, I shifted uneasily on the chair and my eyes were increasingly drawn to the lower grades. Previously, I had figured that I was competing with my fellow brown belts for a place in the first team but now I realized that there were others who were also in the reckoning.

Toru Takamizawa, Cox sensei's old instructor, had said that while training there is no cruelty in karate. He was of the opinion that to hold back with a technique, or purposely miss with a kick or a punch, was to do a great disservice to a fellow student as then there could be no way of telling if a defensive technique needed correcting. Therefore, it was a kindness to strike your training partner, as it was much better to be hit while in the dojo rather than while out on the streets. The YMCA dojo was full of cruel kindnesses that night. On seeing the lower grades partnering the brown and black belts I had expected their blood to be spilt, especially when they were instructed to disregard their natural inclination to retreat as fists and feet flew towards them. But they did as they were told, they stepped in to meet their attackers, and through the fear, to counter the techniques that were thrown (now I was looking at them from the sidelines) with frightening velocity.

Amongst the orange and green belts the level of success varied greatly. Danny Moore, a wiry and tough green belt, was performing well and throwing counter-techniques with unerring accuracy. The Bryan brothers, Mick and Neville, looked sharp, as did Flash, a stick-thin green belt whose smile was the only thing about him that could be described as broad. Don Hamilton, only an orange belt, never missed an opening. He had joined the club at the age of sixteen and had entered the dojo with the cockiness of an accomplished street-fighter. As a boy he had taken on three grown men who had racially abused him and he had turned up at the club with a fraction too much self-assuredness for his own good – but it only took a front kick from one of the black belts to correct his attitude. Don had only been training for two years but he was already looking like an accomplished karate fighter. It was only when Eddie Cox had brought the lesson to an end with the two ceremonial bows did I notice that one of the best green belts was missing. Dalton was an ex-soldier who had joined the club three years previously to hone his fighting skills. I recalled that as a sixteen-year-old I had tried to 'win' my manhood the first time I had encountered him. The sensei had probably thought he had found a remedy for my own cockiness by putting me to fight with Dalton.

I was just out of school and he had recently left the British Army. He had a large physique and his punches were very hard. After several minutes of refusing to be overwhelmed by this outsider, sensei, with a cruel smirk on his face, called an end to the bout. Dalton came over and congratulated me on my tenacity. Little did he know that within those several minutes of fighting he had almost succeeded in rearranging my internal organs. It was an exercise that made me recognize that I was still an adolescent and left me passing blood in my urine for a week. Years later I would be paying an annual visit to a renal specialist and while I cannot say it was all due to Dalton, I think it is safe to assume that he had played a part in the unhealthy state of my kidneys.

The buzz amongst the students in the changing room was due to the news of Dalton getting arrested for armed robbery. It was strange how what happened in the YMCA unwittingly replicated aspects of karate in Japan, where in some minds it is regarded as a low-level fighting art that is indelibly linked with the criminal activities of the yazuka. Perhaps this is due to karate being a fairly direct martial art without the nuances of the more traditional aikido or iaido schools. Also, some private karate dojos were situated in areas of Japanese cities where criminal gangs were located and the type of person attracted to enrol at these schools would have naturally reflected this. The YMCA's dojo was in the middle of a red-light district; the hall was very basic and with very few facilities. The training fee was small – and sometimes it was not even bothered with. The young men who joined the YMCA were automatically drawn from the rougher parts of town: some of them were criminals before they ever started training, while others became criminals once they had mastered, in part, the control of fear and the ability to keep a cool head while under pressure. But at the YMCA no criminal had ever got beyond the rank of brown belt and there seemed to be a lesson in that fact for me and my young friends: get to the rank of black belt and enhance the chances of living a life without the appendage of a criminal record.

But despite his criminal activities and all the pain he had caused me, I had a sneaking regard for Dalton. He was a man of his word and I admired his no-nonsense attitude to life that had made him a popular figure in the dojo. His first brush with the law came when he was arrested not only for a crime that he had not committed, it was a crime that had never taken place. Even though he walked from the court, a free man, the experience embittered him. The type of incident that had pushed Dalton toward a life of crime was happening more frequently. It seemed every week someone I knew had a similar tale about a black man who had been wrongly stopped or arrested by the police. Experiences like Dalton's had helped to spread feelings of distrust and a notion that a whole community was under threat. For men of my age it stoked anger and resentment and put a little spite into the techniques we practised. Therefore, rather than seek the help of the police, people

I trained with increasingly took the law into their own hands. Following the actions of Jerome and Ewart to rid the nightclub of trouble caused by criminal elements, there had been several occasions when the assistance of the YMCA karate club had been sought by people who had been either threatened or burgled. The club's reputation was growing because of events outside of the dojo as well as those actions within it.

Following a couple of katas as part of a warm-down session, the lesson came to an end with the two usual bows from a kneeling position. In Japanese martial arts there is the saying: '*Rei ni hajimari, rei ni owaru.*' It means that the training must begin and end with a bow. It is important for discipline to be maintained within any dojo but particularly when it contains thirty-odd young men imbued with too much pride and too much testosterone. The bows at the beginning of every session signalled that we were entering another world, in which animosity and anger were to be put to one side and within that period between the bows we were followers of bushido. The fact it was a Japanese code also reminded us that our instructors were no longer to be considered our peers while we were in the dojo and that in some way they were merely echoing the strictures that had been laid down by the countless generations of martial artists who had gone before them. Consequently, we submitted ourselves to the type of punishments that in any other context would have been unacceptable to us.

"Some of us must think they don't need to train," Trog muttered as he walked by. There was an ill-founded air of superiority about Trog that got on everyone's nerves, even those of the instructors and a couple of times he had been taught a very hard lesson after questioning a technique that had just been shown to the class. But even in his pain he displayed an attitude that communicated that now he had experienced its effectiveness the instructor now had his permission to show it to the rest of the students. "Shut your big mouth, Trog." I replied. "I wasn't the one fighting like a pansy."

"We'll see who's a pansy next time we spar," the Trog said, in a vain attempt to save face.

Leslie rushed past me on his way to the changing room and said something to me which I did not quite hear. I was too busy watching Ewart rebuking Clinton for his performance against Trog. Ewart made it clear, in no uncertain terms, that he expected better from his younger brother. But talking was not enough for Ewart, he demanded the highest levels of skill and effort from everyone in the dojo – but particularly of those of us who were related to him. I felt uncomfortable watching as Clinton sparred with Ewart. I winced with each punch that struck Clinton's already bruised body. Each blow Ewart dealt was a warning of the consequences of failure.

Once they had finished and Ewart had left, I walked over and placed a hand on Clinton's hunched shoulders when I saw how gloom-laden he was. I asked him what had gone wrong during training.

"Besides Ewart thinking I'm useless?"

"You and everyone else below black belt," I said, in an attempt to offer him some comfort.

He laughed and playfully punched me in the stomach. "I can't seem to get my fighting right," he said, "nothing I do lately seems to work. Trog was all over me today. I just couldn't keep him off."

I felt my eyes water as I tried to mask the discomfort his light tap on my belly had caused me. Fate had definitely smiled on me that night in order to prevent me from training. "Is that all you're worried about?" I said, trying to lighten his mood. "Here's me thinking you were just distracted."

"What do you mean?" he replied, glancing at me quizzically.

"You know, the girls standing on the corner outside and while you were sparring you were wondering how much they would charge a really ugly guy like Trog."

Laughing out loud, we made our way to the changing room. Leslie rushed towards us, pulling dry clothes over his still wet body. He said to me, "Don't forget, tonight we have two nice-looking girls waiting for us. I told them we would pick them up for nine."

I had completely forgotten about the double-date Leslie had

previously made for the two of us. I suspected he had only involved me because the car he had recently bought was not yet roadworthy and he needed a lift. Although I knew Leslie would object, I felt Clinton would benefit from tagging along and as he got changed I told him he needed to come with us for a relaxing night out.

Clinton was chuckling while Leslie was cursing as the three of us finally clambered into my car.

— Chapter Four —

*We shout during a fight according to the
situation. The voice is a thing of life.
Miyamoto Musashi — The Fire Book*

AT NINETEEN I had struck out for independence and got a place of my own, although this was not entirely by choice. On learning that a friend of his was planning to return to Jamaica, my father suggested that I should take over the tenancy of his flat. It was on the twelfth floor of a high-rise block on the other side of town, about five miles from my parents' home. Dad was showing me the door, in a gentle roundabout way, mostly because the house in which I had grown up had become too small for the six of us, particularly as I was the only boy and so had a bedroom to myself. As my three younger sisters became adolescents and had started to bicker in their cramped space, my presence in the home was viewed as problematic.

I did not mind in the least, and Clinton and Leslie positively celebrated when I told them the news – as they still lived with their parents and had notions about turning my second bedroom into some sort of 'love nest'. I made sure that never happened. The flat was empty but for a bed, a wardrobe and an old three-piece suite and I had not got around to putting much more furniture into it. The floor remained uncarpeted and was covered by hard grey vinyl tiles and the only source of heat was an ineffectual two-bar electric fire. My own ideas about using the flat for romantic liaisons had also come to nought. I had recently split up with the girl I had known from school and there was a part of me that felt as empty as my flat. But I turned my life of temporary solitude into an opportunity to train even harder. I used all the empty space as a training area, I ran up and down the flights of stairs rather than use the lift and I went out for either early morning or late evening runs. I pushed myself, just as I imagined my rivals for a first team place were pushing themselves. At the YMCA every member trained on their own but would nearly always deny doing so, it was part of a psychological contest. It was not unusual to hear someone comment that the only training he did was in the dojo – the implication being that any improvement he showed was due to having more natural talent.

But despite having my own place, my lifestyle was not completely independent: on the way back from the factory, I still called in for the meal my mother prepared for me every evening. What I missed most were those Sunday mornings when my father would cook breakfast whilst singing over and over again the few hymns he knew. The smells of fried food and those sounds, from the comfort of my bed, were part of my happiest memories. The aroma of fried bacon became evocative of the times when I was secure within those four walls of the family home.

But the sense of security a middle-class area afforded me had gone. As a small child I had lived in a house that did not even have a bathroom but my parents worked hard so we could move out of the squalor and into a more salubrious neighbourhood. Now I was back to living in a far less affluent suburb – and away from my friends and family. And more troubling than that, I was one of only a handful of black tenants in a locality where the racist National Front was active and in a block of flats where there was a gang of skinheads, who had a reputation for what was called 'Paki-bashing'. I had yet to see any of them, although I had seen 'NF' sprayed onto a few walls, but I was told that they were some-where in the floors above me. But the first incident I had heard

31

about that had some kind of racist motivation was an argument between two white tenants. Karen was a young single mother who had a flat next door to mine. She had returned to the communal laundry room in the basement to find that an impatient young girl had emptied her freshly washed clothes onto the floor so that she could use the machine. Harsh words were exchanged but when the girl made a derogatory remark about Karen's mixed-race child a punch to the mouth brought the heated argument to an abrupt halt. The trouble then escalated when the girl's boyfriend, parents and, finally, the police intervened – but not before the latter had mistakenly come to my door.

One of the policemen had asked me had I encountered any trouble; he did not say what kind but I had an idea of the type of trouble he was referring to. We regarded each other with mutual suspicion, so much suspicion on my part that, rightly or wrongly, I thought that his enquiry was meant to heighten my sense of being under threat.

I did start to wonder if my father's friend had been totally straight about his reasons for leaving the flat but the menacing atmosphere was also something I used to motivate me to train as hard as I could. In the dojo we were often reminded to maintain *zanshin* – an awareness of our opponent – when working in pairs. After the cop had left, I vowed that I would not be caught unawares.

I had not been in my new home a month when that promise I had made to myself was first tested. I was feeling bloated from the huge bowl of Jamaican soup my mom had cooked for me. As mother's do, she had guessed correctly that my flat was still empty of any homely touches and insisted that I took two boxes of items that I thought were mostly junk. I thought the load was too much for me to climb the stairs, so I awkwardly balanced the boxes on one knee as I pressed the lift call button. The doors groaned as they slowly opened. The man who stepped out took me by surprise: he was about my build; height and age; and his hair was cropped short like mine but the colour of our skins were different. I wore the YMCA's blue tracksuit; he was dressed in a skinhead's uniform of a blue denim jacket and jeans that were held up with braces so that the turn-ups barely reached the tops of his shiny Doc Martens.

For a few moments we stared at each other. There was instantly a hatred between us that I could almost taste. The skinhead's eyes communicated that on another day (most likely if he were with his gang) he would have tried to do me physical harm. I responded with a glare that conveyed that I was convinced that if he attacked me I would come very close to killing him. But this was not the right time for him. I wanted to drop the boxes and pummel him for what he represented because I had heard and seen too much about what skinhead gangs had got up to around the town. But they chose their victims well and a man like him would rarely look for violence on a one-to-one basis, unless the victim was much smaller and frailer than I was. He was still staring at me as the lift doors slid shut and I renewed my vow that I would not be caught unawares again.

*

As he had done when I was living with my parents, after the fighting class on Saturdays my cousin Clinton would call during the afternoon and we would go for a run together. We ran for several miles, until we found a patch of ground where we could stretch and throw a few techniques before heading back. But because of my chest injury, after less than a mile I was struggling more than usual to keep up with him. Clinton was a superb athlete, whose long supple legs could keep moving at the same fast pace for many, many miles. I too had made it into the school's track and field team but 400 metres was about as far as I could go competitively. There were many times in keeping up with Clinton that I had suffered attacks of stitch but I had refused to halt and ran through the pain. But what I was suffering right then was far more painful than stitch. Clinton had run another twenty yards before he realized that I was no longer at his shoulder. He looked back and saw that I was bent double before he jogged back to me.

"What's up?" he asked.

It took a while before I could find the breath to answer. Finally, I gasped, "Kick . . . Jerome . . . nurse at work . . . says it's a cracked . . . sternum . . . Don't say anything . . . about it to anyone . . . at the club . . . Okay?"

"Do you think it can heal in three weeks?" Clinton asked, his mind automatically turning to the British Clubs' championships.

"It'll have to," I replied. Clinton wanted to go back to the flat but I insisted that we jogged to a nearby park to practise a few techniques. We pulled on our hand pads and started off by throwing gyakuzuki punches at one another's bodies. I kept my non-punching arm fastened over my solar plexus, while Clinton allowed me to hit him in the stomach. When his turn came, his punches fell six inches short. I told him to hit my forearm as he needed to get his distance right and I needed to know if my arm would provide adequate protection. His first punches were light, too light to see if my arm could absorb fairly heavy impact. "Harder, Clint," I growled at him, "you're punching like a fairy." The next few punches landed with a little more force but I still had to find out what I could take. "No wonder Trog was taking liberties with you," I said to provoke him. His next punch had me shuffling backwards.

"Was that hard enough?"

I grimaced and told him it was.

Back at the flat we discussed the merits of body armour. When karate was first practised in Europe there was little protection for the karateka while sparring. The Japanese instructors had set their faces against protective padding and said that any sort of barrier between the fist and its target made the art of focussing the blow (*kime*) much more difficult to master. In the early days, a few fighters used soccer shin pads tucked inside elastic bandages as it was quite common for a shinbone to come in contact with the bony sharp end of an elbow while sparring. Such an injury made it difficult to walk, never mind train. Some of the instructors in the 'pro-pain' lobby reckoned that such injuries would deaden the nerves in the leg and it was often pointed out that Thai boxers kicked tree trunks to achieve the same effect. Quite simply, there was a widely held opinion that pain was something to overcome and the more frequently karateka experienced it, the sooner they would learn to cope with it. But as Hironori Ohtsuka had done back in the 1930s as he experimented with the idea of karate contests, padding was gradually allowed in European dojos as a training aid during the 1970s, even though some competition rules forbade its use.

But my chest needed protection at a time before body armour (as used by Olympic taekwondo competitors) was readily available. With Clinton's help I put on the bandages Brenda had given me and inserted a bathroom sponge to cover my sternum. I then asked Clinton to punch it. He twisted his mouth as if to signal that I was a damn fool and he gave me a half-hearted punch. "That obviously doesn't work," he muttered, on seeing how much my face had creased with pain. I needed a foam of greater density and it was not long before I was pulling apart a cushion from one of my armchairs.

With the aid of a bread knife I cut the thick foam down to size and stuffed into the bandages. Clinton burst out laughing and made a comment about the attractiveness of my bust size. Not to be deterred, I told him that it would flatten when the bandages were tightened. I imagined the following scene must have been reminiscent of a Victorian lady having the strings in her corset pulled. After having my chest so constricted that I could hardly breathe, I could see that Clinton remained unimpressed. "It won't look so noticeable once I have my gi on," I said, as I went to fetch my jacket.

Clinton reluctantly conceded that if I wore a tee-shirt under my gi the protective padding would not be so obvious. "But why not just say that you're injured, or take a week off?" he asked.

Rivalry within the YMCA club not only made us deceitful about the amount of training we did away from the dojo, it also came as second nature to exploit any perceived weakness. If someone came to train with a bandaged ankle, few in the dojo would have any compunction about hitting it with an *ashi barai* foot sweep. Just as in the streets, there were no favours given in the dojo. If it had been anyone else suggesting that I took time off I would have been suspicious about their motives but Clinton was my closest friend and training partner – and not a rival. "Clint," I warned him, "I'm not saying anything and you've got to promise me that you won't either. Look, the fact that I'm moving around at all means that it can't be too badly cracked, maybe it's just a deep bruise."

I began to take off the bandages and he said, "Those won't work."

"Have you a better idea?"

"Yeah, I think I have," he replied. "I think I got something that will keep the padding in place if you're going to be so stupid as to try and train on Tuesday. That's if you're not so crazy as to try and do the run tomorrow. That would finish you for sure."

I had barely managed a mile with Clinton and on Sunday mornings the club met for a run that was at least six times as far – and then it was followed by an hour of gruelling training in the park. The next run would be the last before the tournament and as much as I hated to admit it, there was no way that I could manage such a run in my state. Despite my temptation to do otherwise, I accepted Clinton's warning and said that I would see him next at the dojo. "Enjoy the run," I said, knowing he would, "and bring that thing with you on Tuesday."

*

I had managed to resist visiting the factory nurse Brenda. While I was tempted to seek her out for another couple of painkillers, I knew she would ask me about the promise to see my doctor that I had failed to keep. There had been many mechanical break-downs to keep the maintenance crew busy and I had neither the time to think about the injury, nor the opportunity to do any sort of practising with Mick. It did confirm to me that while the pain was definitely physical, it was my mental attitude that dictated how much it impaired my movements. By the time of my next visit to the dojo, I was convinced that I was on the mend and I could get through the next training session without too much difficulty.

I was first in the changing room, so I could strap myself up without anyone seeing. After five minutes of light exercises I could feel the bandages loosen and imagined them unravelling altogether during the lesson. I took them off again and waited to see what Clinton would bring me.

Three or four guys had got changed and ambled into the dojo before Clinton arrived. I figured I would now have to put on whatever he had brought in the privacy of the solitary toilet cubicle. "So," I said expectantly, "what have you got?"

He rummaged through his kit bag and my anticipation was heightened with every drawn out second it took for him to find what he had brought me. Finally, he thrust something into my hands. It was not as if I had not seen one before but it still took some time for me to actually work out that Clinton had brought me a bra to wear. I was about to let out a torrent of abuse as he said, "No joke, Ralph, that's what it's designed for. Just put the foam in the titty bags." The sounds of someone approaching had me rushing over and stuffing the bra back into his bag. Weaknesses of the physical sort were not the only ones to be unmercifully exploited at the YMCA; our friend Leslie was a master of finding out some embarrassing fact and then using it as a part of his version of the Chinese water torture. I had seen and heard how he had driven grown men to the verge of tears with his constant taunting. Part of me was convinced that Clinton was not serious and that he was making a point about how stupid I was for thinking that I could train with such an injury. If it ever got found out that I wore a bra, in any circumstance, I would have had to move town, never mind karate club!

A couple of guys dropped their bags and headed into the dojo before I let Clinton know that I did not appreciate his insane offer. "Insane?" he said. "Do you mean more insane than a guy with a broken chest thinking he can train here, of all places? Ralph, buck up your ideas and at least tell Eddie about it and that you can't do any sparring for a while."

I was about to remind Clinton that he was not to mention my injury when Trog walked in from the direction of the toilet cubicle. He greeted us with a broad grin and I immediately worried that he had overheard what Clinton and I were talking about. I decided there and then that I would have to take my chances and train without any protective padding on my chest.

The first hour of training was as strenuous as usual but my chest had not given me any serious trouble. Stretching was followed by the two bows to signal the beginning of the lesson proper. Any latecomers were allowed to train, after a penalty of fifty press-ups on the knuckles, provided they got to the dojo during the preliminary exercises and before the call of "*Sensei ni rei!*"

One of the secrets of the YMCA's success was the manner in which the students were taught how to apply the techniques they learnt while moving up and down the hall in lines. In traditional Wado Ryu karate there are a number of graduated sequences of prearranged fighting techniques that Hironori Ohtsuka had devised. Yakusoku (or sometimes called kihon) kumite involves an attacker and defender in a series of techniques which teaches the basic principles of Wado: irimi (entering); kawashi (avoiding); nogare (escaping); nagashi (sweeping away); and taisabaki (body control). Many similar techniques and footwork are found in other martial arts such as kendo and aikido and I had witnessed some of those principles put into devastating effect when Jerome had disarmed the huge man with the knife. Tatsuo Suzuki then developed ohyo gumite, (semi-free fighting) in which the techniques are more like actual fighting but again both attack and defence are prearranged. Eddie Cox and his fellow senseis developed this further with several forms of sparring in which sometimes the attacks were prearranged but the methods of defence could be a choice of two or three techniques; a prearranged attack to be countered with any technique of the defenders' choice; and then the free exchange of techniques in a controlled fashion that was called 'slow-sparring'. Slow-sparring involved the execution of techniques at less than full speed but this was something of a misnomer when practised by the senior grades. To the untrained eye it still can look very fast when performed by black belts as their eyes and reactions have become so attuned to the movements of the karateka in front of them. In one celebrated case a TV crew had turned up to film Jerome Atkinson and Declan Byrne after the former had become the world heavyweight all-styles champion. Dutifully, the pair slow-sparred but the film crew said their kicks and punches were just too fast. They slowed their techniques but it was not until the fifth take that the cameraman was happy – mostly because Declan Byrne had hit the hard concrete floor so many times in the previous four takes that he could hardly move during the final attempt to get it right.

Cox sensei ordered us to make two lines that faced each other. One side would attack in any way it wished while the other defended – but this time no blocks were allowed and only punches could be used as a counterattack. I paired off with Clinton first and did the attacking. He was back on form and slipped and avoided everything I threw at him before he came back with a flurry of light punches to my head and body. I had my go as the defender until the sensei called out for us to change partners and I was tidying my gi before I looked up to see my new partner was Trog.

As usual, Trog had a smirk on his face. For a man with such a broad and powerful build he was very fast and flexible and was known for his mawashigeri (roundhouse kick) to the head. In a change from his ordinary tactics, most of his attacks were aimed at my body, so I countered with a punch to his head called nagashizuki, a front hand technique which is thrown while one swivels the body to avoid an attack. Even though he was not managing to hit me, I could see just how much force he was putting behind his kicks but I saw this as nothing unusual as we were often reminded of Takamizawa's adage of being cruel to be kind whilst training. It was not until we had swapped roles did I realize what Trog's smirk was all about. As I attacked he concentrated on throwing punches to my body, even though I was purposely covering up and leaving my head unguarded. He must have heard

Clinton and me discussing my injury when we were in the dressing room. We were often told that when facing an opponent that there were two emotions we had to overcome: our own fear and our own anger, as both can make the muscles stiffen and less efficient. I let anger get the better of me and started to attack with even more venom. This was a big mistake as one of the principles of Wado Ryu karate is to make use of an attacker's own power and strength against him. The harder I attacked Trog, the harder his blows were smacking against the damp flesh of my forearms. But I could not stop myself, with each attack I applied as much force as I could muster while I gave out a loud kiai. He came back with counters accompanied by his own kiais; and in this case he who was shouting last was shouting loudest. As it had to do, one his blows finally got through; I could feel his largest knuckle sink in between two of my ribs – but the pain seemed to travel along my bones and converge at my sternum. I moved back to a starting position and realized I was in a predicament, mostly of my own making. If I let up in my attacks, Trog would sense it and claim a moral victory but if I continued to attack with the same intensity – and he hit me again´ – I doubted if there was any way that I could remain on my feet and then his victory would be complete. Hell, I thought, I'm not backing off. This time using the painful lesson I had learned from Jerome, I threw a feint before launching a kick. Trog took the bait but was not so committed to a counterattack as I had been, therefore when the ball of my foot hit his chest he went over onto his back. The results may have looked more spectacular than when Jerome had kicked me – but in falling backwards Trog had taken part of the sting out of the maegeri. Whatever else Trog was, he was a fighter and was quickly on his feet to rush at me with a combination of punches that had me scrambling backwards. I managed to parry every punch – except for the last one. It was not as hard as the one to my ribs but the punch that landed just below my collar bone had my eyes watering. I thought I had made a good job of disguising my yelp of pain as a kiai but it brought me to the attention of the sensei. He watched me attack another two times; I was trying as hard as I could but all strength had drained from me and I could feel myself reacting even though Trog's punches were missing or hitting my arms.

After the final bow Eddie Cox called me to one side and delivered devastating news when he told me that he was ordering me to stop training for a while. I protested but he was insistent. "Ralph," he said, "there's no way I'm letting you train with that sort of injury. I was watching you all the lesson and you're only doing yourself more harm than good. Do a little light stretching at home but you are not training here for two weeks."

I went and got changed; too upset to talk to anyone, especially Clinton, before I headed for home. I was feeling betrayed as well as hurt.

— Chapter Five —

Polish your wisdom; learn public justice,
distinguish between good and evil and study
the ways of different arts one by one.
Miyamoto Musashi — The Water Book

BY SEVEN-THIRTY the factory had wound down, its heavy machinery was now at rest. The slumbering giants would not be roused again until the morning. Everything would remain still except for the occasional shadowy figure of a maintenance worker clambering over the huge presses. Oil can in hand, he would lubricate the bearings that were impossible to get at while the gargantuan machines were in use. The workers who operated these mechanical brutes were mainly immigrants from the Caribbean and the Indian subcontinent. They seemed to know little, and care even less, about the hazards associated with such occupations; despite its perilous nature, the work provided an opportunity to escape from a poverty-stricken life.

When I had first encountered these machines, as a boy straight from school, I was absolutely terrified of them. The department known as the stamp shop was hot, dirty, noisy and dangerous; it was a part of the factory that I thought was very close to hell on earth. It was at this time that my feelings towards my father changed from one of adolescent resentment to a grudging respect. I knew he worked in conditions similar to those I had seen in the stamp shop but up until that point I had not appreciated the sacrifices he had made for his family. He had put food on the table and with my mother, had established some sort of foundation on which my sisters and I could build our lives.

The machine Mick had been working on still refused to work in the correct sequence. He told the rest of the crew what was wrong but clueless and bored, most of us just nodded and hummed as though we were trying to think of a solution.

However, I was thinking more about the training sessions I had to miss. The more I thought about it, the more I convinced myself that someone had told the sensei about my injury so as to sabotage my chances of fighting in the first team at the British Clubs' championships. But my ambitions were not going to be foiled so easily. During the day, Mick and I had sneaked into a deserted area at the rear of the factory to practise combinations of kicks and punches amongst the old disused machinery. I still felt some discomfort in my breastbone but Mick was no Trog: we always kept the techniques light as we were aware that we had to be in a fit state to continue with our work.

As the debate about what was wrong with the machine became more heated, I simply wanted to lay down my tools and get to the YMCA so as to keep an eye on those I figured were my rivals, yet I knew this would have been unacceptable. There was an unwritten rule amongst the maintenance workers that meant we stuck together as a team until a job was finished. But the team's frustration had begun to wear away our solidarity. The mechanics blamed the electrical circuitry and the electricians blamed the mechanical sensors. It was reaching the point that everyone working on the problem began to fear that we might be there for the night. But thankfully, the maintenance engineer in charge of the whole department, finally got the thing going after a bit of nimble finger work. We were too mentally exhausted to cheer.

On the way out I threw a slow, playful gyakuzuki at Mick and he blocked it with soto uke. "Shouldn't you be training tonight?" he asked, immediately sobering my mood.

I told him that I would not make it to the dojo in time and he asked did I want to go to his place for a little training and a bite to eat. Training was always preferable to watching.

Mick's standard of fighting was nowhere near the level of what would be found at the YMCA but what he lacked in ability, he more than made up for in determination. Once we got to his house he suggested that we went for a run to warm up. Such was my competitive streak that I did not like to refuse. That I had the reputation of the YMCA to uphold banished all thoughts of my sternum and before long I was out with Mick pounding the damp streets. Every now and again he would halt and have us doing press-ups on our knuckles before resuming our run. Despite being firm friends, we still felt the need to prove ourselves to one another, or perhaps we were trying to prove which one of us practised the better style of karate.

Our attitudes had their origins in what had happened in Japan when Ohtsuka left Funakoshi to set up his own school many years before either of us was born; it had been akin to a religious schism and its legacy was an attitude that was very similar in nature to sectarian bigotry. In the early days, when the YMCA had travelled to the north of England to enter tournaments organized by Shotokan groups, the team had often fallen victim to unfair refereeing. For a time Shotokan officials would not recognize a roundhouse kick unless it was delivered with the ball of the foot (in Wado Ryu it is normally the top of the foot that does the striking) or a uraken (back-fist) strike which sometimes would be thrown in competition rather than a punch in order to cut down the risk of injury to an opponent's face. When coming up against that sort of officiating some unfortunate competitor normally ended up getting hurt as a frustrated YMCA team member was compelled to give a demonstration of the real power in his kick, or punch. But the YMCA persevered and continued to enter Shotokan tournaments because they liked the spirit for which Shotokan competitors were renowned and an attitude which made them least likely to roll around the mat feigning an injury to secure a win. And luckily for the YMCA fighters there were referees like Terry O'Neill and Steve Cattle amongst the officials. They were genuinely very tough Shotokan men who had competed – and triumphed – in all-styles competitions at international level and had honed their skills on nightclub doors in the rougher parts of Liverpool. Perhaps it was down to confidence in their own abilities that they did not display the partisanship that bedevilled so many karate competitions. Men like O'Neill, Cattle and the great Kanazawa recognized those who were like themselves – true fighting men – and when refereeing a match involving YMCA and Shotokan fighters they always officiated with absolute impartiality.

I was not hung up about styles; I had fought and sometimes lost to fighters from other schools of karate. One of my more memorable fights was a great scrap which I lost to a Shotokan international fighter named Ronnie Christopher and I took such experiences with as much good grace as I could muster. In fact, like the rest of the YMCA team, I respected individuals who had given me a good fight rather than any other style or club. When I had enrolled at the YMCA, I had been unaware of the existence of more than one type of karate; like the vast majority of beginners I had no idea about Wado Ryu, Shotokan, Goju Ryu, Kyokushinkai and the rest. But Mick liked to talk up Shotokan's many strong points and had often dropped a hint about coming to the YMCA to train. It was my concern for his safety (rather than any criticism of Shotokan) that made me point out what I saw as a flaw in a movement or technique that would be mercilessly exploited by the majority of my clubmates. They did, after all, have something of a track record of beating Shotokan fighters who were a little more proficient than Mick. I did not know whether what I saw in his technique was down to Mick personally, or his style, but it made me make up all sorts of excuses about why he could not accompany me to the dojo.

Following our third set of press-ups on the wet road I felt something go 'ping' in my chest. It did not hurt that much but I took it as a warning sign and suggested to Mick that we headed back to his place, preferably at walking pace. Mick could not help but show that he thought he had scored a point. "Maybe I'm practising some inferior style, Mick," I said sarcastically and he laughed loudly as though I had read his mind.

As boxers had found out long before, it can be detrimental to one's performance to continue training at the same intensity right up until the day of a tournament. While the sort of training I was doing with Mick was great for building stamina and spirit, it was a little too intense for me in the run-up to a major championship. Before an important competition the club's six-mile runs on Sunday mornings would cease in favour of a one-mile jog and the hour's training in the park would be replaced with twenty minutes of stretching. Very strenuous training carried the risk of injury and in the period just prior to an event the YMCA team concentrated on speed, technique and sharpening the mind and reflexes.

There was a heavy punch bag hanging in Mick's garage but I resisted the urge to use it as it was as hard as concrete. Instead, I had Mick attack with a few of the techniques commonly used in competition. To the dissatisfaction of many karateka, the rules were becoming increasingly restrictive because of safety concerns (as a result of a few deaths and very serious injuries during competition) and also a hope that karate might one day be accepted as a replacement for boxing as an Olympic sport; apparently, members of the IOC were not keen on the sight of blood. Therefore, it was with some confidence that I could ask Mick to use no more than a half-dozen different moves, knowing that they would represent the majority of techniques I would come up against at the British championships. We spent the next two hours going to and fro and analysing the effectiveness of particular tactics. My chest hardly hurt at all but the pace of training in Mick's garage could not compare with that which was customary in the dojo. When we had finished in his garage we had something to eat while watching a kung fu video and debating if any of what we were watching would work in real life.

"Maybe after the championships, you might ask Eddie if it's all right if I did some training at your club," Mick said, as I was leaving. I had lost count of how many times he had said something similar to me and I was running out of excuses. "Maybe," I replied, "some time after the championships." His face brightened but while walking away I said to myself that, for his sake, it would be a very long time yet.

*

Clinton called to me and I asked him outright if he had 'grassed' on me. He vehemently denied doing any such thing. "Don't think you can take Cox for a fool," he said. "It wouldn't take a genius to work out there's something up with you. And I hope you're not training with your mate at work, Ralph. You've got to ease up and in some way that's going to take more strength than you carrying on training. Rest and you've got some chance of fighting at the championships, carry on with what you're doing and you're letting everyone down, because there's no way you'll be fit."

He had played the loyalty card very well. To be British all-styles clubs' champions would mean so much to the YMCA because all the best teams from other styles and governing bodies would be competing and it would settle any remaining arguments about which was the top club in the whole of Britain. In its travels the YMCA had triumphed over most of them already but this was an event in which the opponents would be consistently of the highest calibre, there would be no easy matches and every one of us had to be at our best. "Yeah," I finally conceded, "you're right. I guess I'm being a bit selfish."

"Stupid was the word I was thinking of," he said.

"Hey," I said, "try and be a bit more graceful in victory."

Before he left, I confirmed the arrangements for our Friday visit to the nightclub. As usual, I would be picking up Clinton and Leslie on the way to the Rising Star but this time there would be another two – more attractive – passengers also hitching a ride.

*

It had taken half a can of WD-40 in order to get my old car to start. The Hillman Avenger, never reliable in the cold or damp, had once again caused me to let out a string of curses which only ceased when the engine finally roared into life. Grim-faced, Clinton was sitting on his doorstep waiting for me. "You're late," he said.

I was still annoyed over the car's starting problems. "I know, I can tell the time," I replied, irritated that he would grumble, considering I was the one who had decided to bring him along, despite Leslie's protests. Three minutes later I turned the car into a quiet residential area and Leslie was out at the first beep of the horn. He slid onto the front seat of my car, wearing his trademark sly smile and exchanged greetings with me but he ignored Clinton. After a short distance I drove into the car park of a tower block, not unlike the one in which I now lived. Leslie seemed more energized than usual and ran to the intercom at the flats' entrance. After the briefest of discussions he returned to us with a wide grin that made me feel uneasy. "The two of them will be down in a minute," he said, as he retook his seat.

"Only two? What am I going to do?" asked Clinton.

"Not my problem," said Leslie. "I wasn't the one who asked you to come out with us in the first place. You and Ralph can share, or you can get out and get yourself a life."

I gritted my teeth: Leslie's harsh remark was more evidence that what remained of our childhood gang was fracturing still further. My cousin Trevor and a couple of his friends were the first to fall away as four of us joined the YMCA; they had neither the inclination nor the necessary discipline to subject themselves to the harshness of karate training. Cousin Errol kept at it for a while but at green belt he discovered he liked cars and girls a lot more than being kicked and punched.

A rap on the glass of my door broke my thoughts and I was surprised to be confronted by a very voluptuous figure straining the seams of a very skimpy garment. Leslie laughed and opened his door before he tilted his seat forward and offered a hand to the two women who clambered onto the backseat alongside a bemused and wide-eyed Clinton. "This is Ruth," said Leslie, as the bigger of the two got in. She stood at least six inches taller than Leslie. Her friend was small in comparison; it was the first time I had laid eyes on her but she made an immediate impact. Her tight white dress hugged her body and contrasted with her cool dark skin. The long braided hair complimented her angelic face. "And this is Cleo," Leslie added, before he retook his seat.

It took a while for me to get the car moving. Whatever else about Leslie's shortcomings, he was a truly amazing master of psychology – and these were not even the same girls we had taken out on our previous double-date. Just as he could get under a man's skin and have him bawling out in frustration, he could also charm so many good-looking (and tall)women into doing exactly what he wanted. He made use of this gift during his competitive career to gain a psychological advantage over his opponents, once getting a world champion so worked up that by the time Leslie met him on the mat he was already a beaten man.

I was looking into the rearview mirror for a glimpse of Cleo when Leslie said, "Right, let's head for the Rising Star."

The presence of two such young and attractive women had the three of us competing over which one of us could hold their attention for the longest. Of course, Leslie's charisma meant that he was winning and he had all of us in stitches. But the laughter came to an abrupt halt when he shouted at me to stop the car. I slammed on the brakes, frantically looking around and half-expecting to see a cyclist or a pedestrian sprawled out in the road. Without a word of warning, Leslie was out of the car and running across the road to a bus that had just pulled up to a stop. It was then I saw who had attracted Leslie's attention. All of us watched in silence as Leslie raced down the aisle of the bus, before, in one motion, he swung on one of the hand rails and kicked a young man in the head. There was a brief flurry of kicks and punches and the next we saw of Leslie was as he sauntered back towards my car. "C'mon, Ralph," he said nonchalantly, "drive."

Cleo ruined the angelic image I had of her by letting out a string of profanities as she demanded to know what was going on. For the remainder of the journey, the girls did not so much as utter a word but I could tell that they were unsure if it had been wise to accept Leslie's invitation to go clubbing with us.

I knew exactly what had happened and why. I had spotted the young man at the bus stop as Leslie had run across the road. He was the ex-boyfriend of a girl Leslie's charm had lured away. Not being brave enough to take out his frustrations on Leslie, he had made threats of violence and stalked the girl – or so Leslie had told me. But like the two girls in the back of my car, I was not impressed by Leslie's course of action. There had been more than a small element of showing off in the way he had gone about things.

After reluctantly taking turns to dance with the three of us, the girls made out that they were going to "powder their noses" and slipped away. Leslie did not notice, he was too busy talking to the likes of my cousin Trevor and his friend Albert and I knew by how they were laughing that he was describing the incident on the bus. Up until then I had liked to think that any violent actions of a YMCA member outside the dojo were not only justified but admirable. The club we were spending a night in was a testament to the good things karate could produce. Such was the Rising Star's reputation for now being trouble-free that coach loads of people made round trips of hundreds of miles to spend a Friday or Saturday night at the club. I saw a noble quality in those YMCA men who sorted out a gang who had defrauded a blind woman of her savings; in the colleague who had saved a life by knocking out the three guys with knives who had just left a man without his spleen; and in the black belt who had beaten a gang leader and ensured that he would enter a plea of guilty for his crimes, as his violent reputation – for grievous bodily harm and rape – had previously intimidated witnesses into not coming to court to give evidence against him.

The horrified expressions of the two young women as they sat on the backseat of my car stayed with me; like them, I figured that I had not witnessed anything very noble that night.

— Chapter Six —

You must not be influenced by the opponent.
Train diligently.
Miyamoto Musashi — The Wind Book

I HAD RESTED from training for almost two weeks but I had become so used to exercise that it had become like a drug for me and without it I felt lethargic and dull. So I did not go into 'withdrawal', I had continued to stretch my hamstrings as I moved around my flat because I was not one of nature's most flexible creatures – but I did not count that as proper training as I had not broken into a sweat.

When I finally returned to the dojo to train once again, I detected that there was something different about the atmosphere: with only a few days to go to the British championships there was an air of anticipation, rather than apprehension. Excluding myself, everyone looked as fit and as prepared as they could be. Confidence was at its normally high level: the YMCA entered every tournament expecting to win. All that was left now was the selection of the teams. I prepared to hear my name amongst those who would make up the second team but the sensei simply announced all the names of those he wanted to report to the dojo on the morning of the championships.

*

51

The British Karate Federation Clubs' championships were to be held at the Aston Villa Leisure Centre in Birmingham – not much more than twelve miles away – and we had the relative luxury of setting off at 9.00 a.m., instead of at the crack of dawn, as we had to do when travelling to tournaments as far away as Cumbria or Crystal Palace.

As usual, the schedule was unravelling and half an hour past the planned departure time I continued to stand, with several others, on the corner – where young women had touted for business only hours before. Despite my irritation with the late-comers, I carried on with preparing myself mentally for the upcoming contest and refrained from indulging in the teasing carried out by Leslie, who usually targeted the most nervous-looking amongst us.

I did feel apprehensive but I still had a positive frame of mind as I had prepared as well as I could despite my injury. It was usual for me to abstain from all my usual vices and have no less than eight hours sleep the night before. In the morning I would always eat a considerable breakfast before setting out, as usually I would not eat for the rest of the day. But the most important part of my preparation was in the hours before a competition, when I always visualized winning.

Another advantage of the tournament's venue being so close by was that there would be no arguments about whose turn it was to drive. Normally, there would have been a heated debate that usually started with the better-off amongst us giving many reasons for why their pristine cars could not make a long journey and then electing someone else to subject their vehicle to the wear and tear.

As the last of the team members arrived, Leslie offered to take me and a few others in his recently acquired Mark II Ford Escort that he had at last made roadworthy. But the invitation was not extended to Clinton, who had wandered off and stood beside his brother Ewart's car. He stood silent and motionless. I thought he was doing so because he did not want to be beholden to Leslie. But in hindsight, I now realize it was another warning about the changes taking place within my cousin and closest friend.

We arrived late in Birmingham but the event, in common with almost all karate tournaments, was running behind schedule. There was a buzz from other competitors as we walked into the changing room and whispers of our arrival echoed along the walls that were lined with white ceramic tiles. Pretending not to notice the stir we had caused, we began to change into our karate gis. Fighters can be very superstitious and although no one at the club would admit to any such thing, it was not difficult to see it in those getting changed. Some would remove clothing in a set order or tie their coloured belts in a particular manner. I would never allow my shin and foot pads or my hand-mitts to be washed no matter how dirty or bloodstained they became. To do so would have diluted their acquired magic.

All the top competitors knew each other and some of them came over to greet the senior members. Like so many of the second team, I was only considered worthy of the briefest of nods, it was the type of greeting that said: '*Yeah, I've seen you fight, you've got promise but you're not there yet.*' I had been trained to go into a bout expecting to win and with this came a certain amount of arrogance and, along with the rest of the second team, I viewed most fighters from other clubs as our inferiors. While any conceit or boastfulness in victory was frowned upon, there can be no room for humility in the mind of a competitor who wants to win: he has to enter a bout confident in his own abilities and that he will emerge as the winner of any he fight he enters.

When we entered the cavernous sports hall, it seemed to us that the other clubs had collectively conjured up the theory that if they went out of their way to shake our hands and wish us luck we would go easier on them. I would have respected them more if they had just come out and said what they felt: '*I hope I have it in me to give your backside a good kicking today.*'

The few fighters we did not take exception to when they greeted us before the fighting began were from Toxteth in Liverpool. They were genuinely pleased to see us and took pride in associating themselves with our club to the point that they would come and support the YMCA once their team had been eliminated. There was an affinity between us – despite them practising Shotokan – based on the most tenuous of grounds: that of skin colour. I was intrigued by this club as all its members were from one of the oldest black communities in England. Unlike our parents, their forebears were born in England, they spoke with a 'Scouse' accent, their skin tones were various shades of light brown and it was obvious their parents and ancestors were a mixture of black and white and every shade in between. I detected that they felt a sense of alienation from British society that was similar to that experienced by people of my background, who were still perceived as relative newcomers to Britain's shores. What separated these guys from white Liverpudlians was not so much the physical results of their melanin levels but the different consciousness it produced. When listening to them talk of the type of segregation mind-set that prevailed in their city, I thought about the similar attitudes I had become aware of in the area in which I now lived.

When I took a seat that overlooked the fighting areas that were made up of vibrant blue and red *tatami* (mats) and saw the number of fighters that had travelled from every part of Britain, the scale of the event produced an anxious jabbing pain in my gut. Our first team was amongst the favourites to take the title of British Clubs' champions but there were several other teams, with international competitors within their ranks, that were also strong contenders.

As even more fighters entered the hall, Eddie Cox ordered us to take ourselves to the far end of the bleachers so we could be away from all the distractions and relax. While some of the others continued to limber up, I lay down and closed my eyes as I reflected on the long road travelled in getting to this point – and the sacrifices we had all made for the YMCA. The anxious pain in my gut began to fade and before long my mind began to wander and I recalled my very first bout as a fifteen-year-old novice yellow belt.

In 1977 karate competitions were still a very tough and macho affair: women and children were precluded from fighting and could only vent their competitiveness in the kata events. But at fifteen years old I was fairly big for my age and, as a result of the bare knuckle fights I'd had, I was confident that I was ready to enter a fairly small local tournament. It was not difficult for me to recall the fear I felt as I stood on the fighting area for the first time. There was a grown man standing across from me and I remembered my knees shaking as I tried to give off an air of confidence by staring at my opponent – until his intimidating scowl forced me to avert my eyes toward my toes. I was still looking down when the referee called for the bout to begin with a shout of *'Hajime!'* Screaming like a banshee, the brown belt raced toward me and threw a heavy front hand punch which I evaded – but I failed to see the following two-punch combination. There was a thud on my forehead and suddenly I was on my backside listening to the crowd cheering wildly. Through watering eyes I looked across to Eddie Cox, who just bared his teeth and clenched his fist. I clambered to my feet and made my way back to my line. My opponent stood red-faced and snarling as the referee awarded him a *wazari* (half point) before the bout resumed.

Again he rushed at me but aware of his tactics, I retreated faster than he advanced and several times I was chased over the boundaries of the fighting area. This continued until the crowd booed and the referee warned me that I was at risk of being disqualified for not fighting. Eddie Cox crouched at the side of the area and called me over. The referee promptly waved him away but not before he whispered to me, "Someone just told me that the guy's a member of the National Front!"

I returned to my line. My opponent rushed forward to finish me off. Overcoming my fear and the natural inclination to retreat, I pushed forward, determined to meet him halfway. Squeezing my eyes shut, I punched as hard as I could and felt the impact travel down my arm – while simultaneously I heard a sickening impact amid groans from the crowd. I opened my eyes to catch the last of his descent to the floor, blood oozing from his mouth and nose. The referee restrained him as he temporarily lost his composure, as well as his senses. He struggled to tear away the blood-soaked rag from under his chin and I swallowed hard at the thought of what he might do to me when the bout restarted but to my great relief I was promptly disqualified. Walking from the area, I saw Eddie Cox laughing to himself and I knew then that he had probably lied about the political inclination of my opponent. I had lost but defeat had tasted strangely sweet at that moment.

My eyes opened as a hum of excitement filled the building. Over the tannoy one of the officials called for the coaches to submit the fighting orders of their teams. As I got to my feet, Eddie Cox beckoned me over to him and that pain in my gut came back again. I anticipated that he was about to tell me that I had been relegated to the reserves of the second team because of the training sessions I had missed. "Ralph," he said, "you'll be fighting number three for the first team."

The surprise left me barely able to talk. "Do you think I'm ready?" I mumbled, as the first feelings of self-doubt crept in. "Is Declan injured or something?" I had expected that Declan Byrne would retain his place in the first team upon his return after a year in Ireland, especially when he had joined in with the fighting classes. But unknown to me, he had told Eddie that he no longer felt the urge to compete. He had boxed with some success while he was away and had become even more disillusioned with the changes in the rules of competition karate which further restricted the amount of contact a competitor could make. Along with many others, he was of the opinion that these alterations were diluting a combat system's effectiveness. Eddie Cox smiled. "No," he replied, "he isn't injured, he agrees with Jerome and Ewart that you're ready for the first team. Just do your best."

"And Clinton?" I asked.

"He's going to be the first reserve, okay?"

"Okay," I mumbled, suppressing my urge to cheer out loud. This was the moment for which I had endured years of mental and physical discomfort. But there was no time for any celebration – now I had to prove to myself, and to others, that I was worthy to line up alongside some of the best karate fighters in the country.

As the day progressed, the team advanced much as predicted. Win after win, my confidence in my new role grew. Drawing strength from the others, I felt totally at home fighting at the number three position as opposed to fighting number one for the second team, where there was far more pressure to get the team off to a good start.

Conceitedly, I felt surprised that the second team had not only survived without me but were performing better, much better, than anyone had anticipated. Danny Moore, Don Hamilton, the Bryan brothers, Trog, Leslie and Flash were beating teams that were made up of far more experienced fighters. By the evening, both YMCA teams had progressed to the semifinals. No one dared utter the possibility of the two teams making it to the final for fear of breaking the spell.

Throughout the elimination rounds, Jerome and Ewart, fighting in positions one and two, formed formidable opposition for any team. Neither of them lost a bout and it was hard to recall if any of their opponents had even scored a point against either of them. That changed somewhat when the YMCA fought in the first semifinal. The opposition was a team coached by a man who had trained with Eddie Cox at the Temple Karate Centre in Birmingham. We regarded his team as our inferiors, a 'competition' club, whereas the YMCA trained for combat first and only later were students introduced to the idea of fighting within rules.

Jerome had already gone out and won his fight in his usual efficient no-nonsense manner, when Ewart, in his overly confident way, strolled lethargically onto the mat. It was evident he regarded his opponent with disdain. His bout started with the less experienced fighter moving around and feinting attacks in order to draw a reaction. Ewart sometimes used a style of fighting in which he planted himself on one spot, head slightly tilted to one side, almost trance-like, like a gangly carnivorous insect waiting to strike at its prey with lightening speed. Suddenly, his opponent feinted another attack and when it again drew no response he followed up with a mawashigeri jodan (roundhouse kick to the head) that slapped Ewart hard on the side of his face. The referee could not award an *ippon* fast enough, such was his delight.

Ewart's arrogance, on and off the mat, had won him few friends. There were many, even amongst his admirers, who wanted him taken down a peg or two. A great roar went up as the referee's hand shot skywards to indicate a full point had been awarded. I began to worry that Ewart's dented pride was about to get him disqualified as he sought vengeance, leaving all the pressure on me to re-establish the lead. From behind me I heard Leslie making no attempt to hide his amusement: he could tell what was to follow. The fight only lasted another thirty seconds. Ewart scored three full points, the last one an excessively powerful punch to the solar plexus that folded his opponent as if he were made of paper. He returned to the team still scowling and when he glared at me I understood his unspoken command: nothing but an emphatic victory would suffice.

I was to face their best competition exponent. He had won several tournaments and had a reputation for being cunning and cagey. In many ways he epitomized the nature of his club: point-scoring was everything. The contrast in the ethos of the two clubs was illustrated when he had once made the mistake of visiting the YMCA and asking Declan Byrne to spar with him; it had been a fighter versus a competitor and he never returned to repeat his error of judgment.

My opponent started the bout by moving forward aggressively to intimidate me. I immediately reacted with a counterpunch that he just about evaded. As my fist brushed the side of his head, his eyes betrayed a sudden hesitance. I pressed on, combining feet with fists in my attack. In desperation he lashed out with an open hand and caught me squarely in the mouth, pushing my upper lip against the sharp edges of my teeth. The referee halted the match and called for the doctor to examine the small gash at the edge of my mouth. The doctor placed a plaster on the wound as he announced that the cut would have to be stitched but it could wait until after the bout. The referee asked if I was okay to continue. I nodded, as I was sure I would have my opponent's measure once the bout restarted. The referee turned and gave a private warning about proper control to my opponent who then raised an apologetic hand in my direction. I merely glowered at him in response.

The delay in the resumption of the bout was agonizing for me. I felt embarrassed that I had been caught with a technique that had caused me a disproportionate amount of damage when compared to its feeble execution. All I needed was the opportunity to make amends.

Sweating profusely, I worked hard, perhaps too hard, to land a technique but he wouldn't stand and fight me and I failed to register a score. A bell sounded and a disembodied voice announced there were thirty seconds remaining. Again I attacked and he retreated. Determined to win, I sprang forward and delivered a solid punch that landed just below his throat. He yelled out and confused me as I was sure the blow had landed away from his windpipe. Holding his fist in the air, he raced back to his line. The referee at first appeared confused, before he awarded a half point – to my opponent! Shocked, I looked back to my team, having no idea of what technique he was supposed to have landed on me. With only a few seconds left, he easily avoided my desperate attacks and won the bout.

The two remaining YMCA fighters, Hugo and Chester, won their fights, giving us a four-to-one victory but as I made my way over to the doctor to get my mouth stitched I felt deflated. Declan Bryne took the time to give me a few words of encouragement. "You learn more from your losses than you do from your wins," he said, slapping my shoulders and drawing an admonishing glare from the doctor. "Don't worry, you were the better fighter but he conned the referee. That kind of carry-on is why I packed up competing. When you've finished here, Ewart wants to see you."

He wandered off to watch the other semifinal in which our second team was facing the Shukokai club coached by Eddie Daniels. When the doctor had finished with me, I hesitated about going over to see Ewart. The feeling of dejection brought on by my defeat remained and, as I walked toward my cousin, Declan's words repeated over in my mind: "You learn more from your losses."

To my surprise, Ewart was more reassuring than critical and told me that I had fought well all day. Like Declan, he thought my more experienced opponent had kidded the referee. It was approaching midnight as we went back into the almost empty arena for the final. Most of the spectators had already started their long treks home, back to towns and cities across England, Scotland and Wales once their teams had been eliminated. We were to face the Shukokai team in the final which included Livi Whyte, another Jamaican fighting for Britain, who had been a runner-up in the 1980 world championships. He was a popular man with the YMCA: tough; uncompromising but always fair. By the time the teams lined up for the final I had already worked out where I had gone wrong in my only loss of the day. I knew my opponent but I had failed to block that out from my mind and unwittingly I had made allowances for his style – but that meant he had gained a psychological advantage and I had not fought in my usual way.

The next few minutes were a blur because I fought my final bout of the tournament in exactly the way I had been trained to do: without conscious thought and thereby allowing my body to react in the manner in which it had been conditioned over many years of practise. At the end of the bout the referee raised his hand in my direction and with that the YMCA had an unassailable lead.

The warm water cascading from a showerhead was the next thing I remembered. The banter in the changing area was of Jerome's fight with Livi Whyte. It had been the fight of the championships. Jerome and Livi were friends and colleagues in the British team and knew each other very well. The Shukokai champion was a large man of immense strength and deceptive speed and the fight had ebbed and flowed until a superbly timed front-hand punch from Jerome had upended the oncoming Livi and put more than 220 pounds of muscle onto the flat of his back. The YMCA teams had come first and third in the British Karate Federation Clubs' championships and even our fiercest rivals had to now concede that we were the best karate club in Britain.

— Chapter Seven —

know the smallest things and the biggest things;
the shallowest things and the deepest things.
Miyamoto Musashi — The Ground Book

THE MAIN BOILER lay dormant and awaiting its annual summer refurbishment. It stood mostly obscured by shadows in an isolated small building that was a small distance from the main factory. An old mattress positioned on a mezzanine above and to the back of the boiler was the ideal location for what Mick Davies called 'the retreat'. Impossible to see from the front of the boiler house, it was a site where a select few recovered from a night out at a party, or rested bruised and aching limbs, or simply evaded work. I intended to stay right there for the afternoon after a very tiring morning.

The day had started badly. A charge of adrenalin and the visions of victory had kept me awake for most of the night and I had only nodded off in the early hours. My alarm clock woke me with a jolt and, for the first time, I felt exactly where my opponents' blows had landed on my body as I eased my way out of bed. It was a small source of consolation that my sore mouth distracted me from the dull ache in my chest. But as the adrenalin had dissipated, I was left not only feeling pain but also drained of any enthusiasm for work; it was if I had awoken from an exciting dream and then stepped into someone else's drab and mundane life.

Mick couldn't get enough of the stories of the championships, including the one about how I got the stitches in my mouth. He found that one to be a great source of entertainment but he was bewildered at how low-key I played such an achievement and he constantly scolded me for not bringing in the winners' trophy for everyone to see. It was a tradition in the factory for the workers to bring in any sort of award they had won – usually they were for fishing or pigeon racing – and put them on display in the canteen. Finally, I had to put his mind at ease by revealing that it was more than likely that the local evening newspaper was to publish a photograph and report of the YMCA's victory during the week. It was a source of irritation for Mick that the YMCA had shunned publicity for so long and he had often commented that if his club had achieved only a fraction of our victories the local newspapers and the various martial arts magazines would have been bombarded with reports of the triumphs at almost every major karate tournament in Britain. But it was not the way of the YMCA to court publicity. I did often wonder about the wisdom of such a strategy, especially when it seemed that every week I was reading of boastful karate instructors whose egos were only matched by their inflated, often self-awarded, grades in a magazine or local newspaper. From very early on, Eddie Cox and the other senior members had decided on a course that relied on actions speaking louder than words. At the YMCA, victories were accorded the briefest of handshakes when back at the dojo – although a first win by a junior member was usually given a mention at the start of the following session – and then it was on with the training, the grinding and repetitive training.

"That means everyone will see you," said Mick, on hearing of the probable visit by the local press.

"Only if they buy the newspaper," I said.

"Well then," he said, as though I had just proved his point, "you might as well bring in the trophy tomorrow and give us all a look."

I refused. The last things I needed were questions regarding the 'karate chops' that featured in '*Hai Karate*' aftershave adverts, or the supposed martial arts expertise of David Carradine, star of the *Kung Fu* TV series. By lunchtime I was struggling to keep my eyes open, prompting Mick to suggest that I should spend the afternoon in the seclusion of 'the retreat' while he covered for me.

Once I lay on the grimy mattress I found it hard to doze off. As I had done in my own bed, I replayed the fights of the previous day. It was only the cut in my mouth that caused me to feel anything less than total satisfaction about how the day had gone: I had fought with – and against – the cream of karate competitors, not only in Britain but possibly in Europe. And I had acquitted myself well, although I knew that I still had a way to go to be ranked along with the very best. Next to the mattress was a stash of Mick's ageing martial arts magazines. I found out one from 1976 and again read over an article that then rated the YMCA only joint third in a subjective league table of the top fighting clubs in the country. The victory at the British Clubs' championships was the culmination of five years of hard work to prove that we had been the number one club all along.

There was also a magazine that contained an article on 'race'. Because of the proliferation of black champions in the martial arts, it tried, in pseudoscientific terms, to explain why black fighters were more suited to karate than their white counterparts; citing everything from longer black limbs infused with twitch fibres, to eyes being spaced further apart to give better peripheral vision. As far as I was concerned, it was an article that was riddled with backhanded compliments which were calculated to reinforce racist stereotypes.

In the past, the question of race had periodically cropped up between Mick and me. He was inclined to believe the not-so-natural selection explanation, claiming the slave ships sailing across the Atlantic had weeded out the weak for shark food, leaving the slave masters to increase their chances of breeding physically superior beings by cultivating stronger specimens from those who had survived the arduous voyages. I told him it sounded like he had got most of that stuff from the '*Roots*' TV series. But I did not take offence at Mick's views, as I had heard similar arguments raised by black people I knew. I countered with the argument that it was more nurture than nature and the environment played a large part in why, like so many of their boxing counterparts, many karate champions were black. After all, teams from the Caribbean or Africa were not winning world championships; the top teams in international karate competitions were Britain, The Netherlands and France, all of which contained a high proportion of black men who were now living and training in Europe. To me it was about the opportunity to train with the best teachers, as well as the circumstances in which they had grown up, that had led to the proliferation of so many great black fighters, whether in martial arts or boxing. Declan Byrne was a case in point: although his skin colour was different to that of his colleagues, he had a lot in common with the rest of the YMCA in that he was of immigrant stock and had spent most of his life in one of the roughest council estates in the town. A big factor in Declan's success at karate was an attitude that such an upbringing can create – but he was the first to admit, for many young black men there was also the added factor of racism which could be manifested in anything from daily name-calling to random physical attacks. It was in this kind of hostile atmosphere that many people were forced to confront aggression and think about defending themselves. It was the added dimension of racism that propagated a mind-set which must have been similar to the one that was found amongst the young men who had trained in Japan's dojos before World War II: a martial art for them was not a sport, nor merely a method of keeping fit, for some it had become a matter of life and death.

Top-level instruction from Japanese karateka, who were then amongst the best in the world, also played a part in Britain's success. But, ironically, it was the latent racism within Japanese karate that had made the British team so successful in international competitions, from the mid-1970s right up until the 1990s. After a brief period of condescension in the 1960s, in which there was an attitude that the gaijin student did not possess the innate qualities, nor the martial arts tradition to really learn karate, the Japanese then set the bar so high to achieve a black belt that in many cases a European third dan ended up having a far greater range of techniques and knowledge than his Japanese equivalent. And yet, when given the choice, many clubs in Britain chose a Japanese instructor to do their grading examinations, as it had been so firmly implanted into the subconscious that the belts they awarded were somehow 'more authentic'. Japan's defeat in World War II also remained an influence on how some instructors taught their art. Once, when slightly worse for drink, a Japanese instructor confided in Eddie Cox that he would never teach an American or English karateka all he knew. They could speak the language, profess a love for the culture, even marry a Japanese and train diligently but there was no way he would impart to them the *ogi* (secret techniques) of Wado Ryu. Another irony only struck me after years of training: many of my peers had become involved in karate as a reaction to the racism they faced on a day-to-day basis and yet many dojos were not the sanctuaries from intolerance they had sought but rather they were often hothouses of prejudices based on grades, style of karate, nationality and race.

*

A couple of days later there was a pleasant surprise waiting for me at my parents' home when I called in one evening: there was a letter informing me that I had been selected to attend trials for selection for an England against Scotland match at under-21 level. I could hardly eat my dinner fast enough before I hurried to Clinton's house.

I found him lying under an old Ford Escort he had bought. His brother Ewart was a Ford mechanic and had told him not to buy it but Clinton spurned the good advice. I told Clinton of the letter but he stayed under the car and grunted that he had received one too. The sound of banging and scraping of metal continued. I had anticipated a different reaction: at first I had been fearful that my selection might provoke some envy but then I quicky discounted the thought as Clinton had never been jealous of any of my successes, in fact he shared in them as I would not have achieved much without him as my training partner. But when I heard that Clinton had also been picked for the trials I immediately expected more of an excited response, in which we would plan a training schedule together. When he finally emerged from underneath the old car, I saw a strange look in Clinton's eyes that I had not noticed before and it disturbed me. It was distant and it was disengaged. I was not sure what to do so I playfully punched him on the shoulder as I congratulated him, hoping it would bring him out of some sort of trance. Clinton looked at his shoulder and then slowly up into my face. He blinked and as if slowly waking, a smile started to spread across his face. "Well," he laughed, "getting selected can't be no big thing, even Leslie got a letter."

I was still feeling a pang of concern for my cousin. "But you're feeling all right, Clint?"

He gave me a puzzled frown and gently poked my chest. "Better than you." He picked up his tools and said, "Come on, let's go inside and work out how we're going to fit in some extra training."

— Chapter Eight —

*Many things cause a loss of balance. One
cause is danger, another is adversity and
another is surprise.*
Miyamoto Musashi — The Fire Book

I HAD ARRIVED early for the first class on Thursday evening.
During the previous session I had been told to turn up for the
junior class, which was for beginners and those students who were
younger than fifteen, to help with their instruction. Through
the door of the dojo I saw an ill-at-ease, wiry man pacing the floor.
"Ralph, hurry up and get changed!" shouted a relieved Eddie
Cox, "there's a man here who wants to take a photo."

Once I had my gi on, I hurried back into the dojo. Reticent about
publicity, none of the senior members had bothered to turn up
for the photo shoot so it was left to Don Hamilton, Mick Bryan,
Trog and one of the younger students to line up with me and our
sensei to proudly show off the British Karate Federation Clubs'
Championship trophy to the readers of the local evening newspaper. The camera's flash lit up the hall half a dozen times before the
photographer produced a notebook and took Eddie Cox to one
side to ask a few questions about the tournament and those who
were present for the photograph. Unused to such media attention,
we gawked at our sensei and the newspaper man until Eddie Cox
looked over and called out, "Mr Robb, please warm up the class."

Trog was not happy as I put the class through a series of stretching routines. He was much more supple than anyone else present and may have been a better choice but I was the higher grade. Trog still had an attitude that communicated he was of the opinion that the position given to me in the first team had been rightfully his, even though I had vindicated my sensei's faith in me with my performances at the championships.

This was my first attempt at giving instructions and I was amazed at how uncoordinated the movements of the beginners were – and yet I had performed the same exercises in a similar awkward fashion only five years before. The changes to my body and mind were incremental over the years of karate training and it was only after being confronted with the ungainly novices did I realize just how much I had changed.

The sensei returned and took the bow to formerly begin the training session and as I was the most senior student present he told me to put the class through the basic techniques. He was throwing me in at the deep end: up until then I had simply followed instructions and never analysed the principles that lay behind them. It was then I grasped how much of a learning experience teaching karate is, as I did my best to explain how to perform a simple punch, the importance of breathing properly and how a kiai (shout) is used to enhance the power of a technique, in a manner similar to that of field athletes and weight-lifters as they expel air during a moment of intense exertion. But with the sensei – and Trog – scrutinizing my performance I was becoming flustered as I tried to put over what I wanted the students to perform. I was glad when I was finally relieved of my duties. As I joined the rest of the students, out of the side of his mouth, Trog said, "You were confusing yourself, never mind the rest of us."

"Yeah," I replied, "like the time when my foot in your chest seemed to confuse you."

By the time the junior class had ended only a quarter of the normal number of seniors had turned up. Despite the discipline in the dojo, in reality there is no compulsion in the martial arts.

No one forces us to go training, we make the choice to do so – and as Hironori Ohtsuka said: the first opponent we must overcome is ourselves. The black belts turned up and offered a series of lame excuses about why they had missed the photo shoot. It had taken a concerted effort by every member, and not just the seven fighters who had made up the first team, to secure the victory and some were obviously still feeling the effects. But by turning out for training the black belts set an example for the rest of us. Each one of the senior grades had their own personal ambitions to drive them on; with so many titleholders in the club it meant that no one could rest on their laurels. Jerome Atkinson was the most outstanding example of this. He had won his first national and European Wado Ryu titles as a brown belt but he realized he needed a change in his training and fighting style to go up a level and win a national all-styles title; and once he had experienced fighting at the 1980 world championships he became aware that his training regime had to be refined yet further if he were to succeed at the very top level. In many ways, he was reprogramming his reflexes and 'muscle-memory' and was a model of extraordinary single-mindedness.

But it seemed some were taking longer than others to recover from the British championships. Clinton and Leslie were amongst the missing and I worried that their call-up for the under-21 trials had made them complacent. Clinton's absence caused me the most anxiety: he was my training partner and I felt it was my responsibility to get him back on track.

*

Clinton was underneath his old Ford again. He had been working on it almost every day in the two weeks since he had bought it and the car had yet to move from the front of his house. Clinton was nothing if not determined but to me it was like trying to breathe life into a body that was long dead. I had driven by his place to see if he wanted a lift to the Saturday morning fighting class but the moment I spotted him I knew he would be too busy with his car to come training. Cursing him and the car, I decided to save my breath and pressed on for Leslie's house.

Leslie's parents were on holiday in Jamaica and, because of previous experiences, when I rang the bell I was unsure of what I would find on the other side of the door. "Quick, come in," he said, eyes furtively shifting from side to side. As he closed the door behind me I noticed how tired he looked and that his clothes were askew as if he had hastily dressed. It did not take me long to work out that he had company, it turned out to be the tall girl to whom we had given a lift to the nightclub with her friend Cleo. After a brief moment of wondering about what girls saw in him and how the hell he had won her around, I asked Leslie if he were coming training and he looked at me as if I had just asked a very stupid question. "But look, Les," I protested, "we have to get back into the groove. We've got the trials coming up, remember."

He was laughing as he said, "Next week, Ralph, we'll start next week. I'm just letting the injuries heal before I get back into serious training."

I drove to the dojo berating both Clinton and Leslie's lapses in dedication but part of me was regretting that I had not asked Leslie about Cleo; perhaps my commitment would be waning too if I had such an attractive distraction in my life.

The fighting class was exactly that. After the customary warm-up exercises there followed an hour of sparring, starting off slow and light but normally finishing very fast and very hard. It still attracted karateka from throughout the area who were looking to improve their fighting skills. It must have been a daunting prospect for them, particularly for the visiting black belts who often found themselves struggling with the green belts – and at the end of the line there were the more proficient and merciless black belts waiting for them. After watching the team win the British championships, a brown belt had travelled from Birmingham to train with us. He bowed while politely asking Eddie Cox if he could join the class. He was at least six-foot-four but his suit had either shrunk or he had borrowed it from a far smaller karateka. His first mistake was to give off an air of timidity and a little fear – the very things that should not be shown when entering a combat situation. How much more fearful he would have been if he had seen the expressions of those who were looking on: we were like a pride of hungry lions who had just spotted our next meal. The trouble the brown belt had taken to visit the YMCA dojo should have been seen as a compliment but for the majority of the low and middle grades it was an opportunity to prove themselves. Trog, as usual, was the most vocal. To the group of green belts around him he said loudly, "The bigger they are, the harder they fall!"

And the tall brown belt did fall many times during that morning's session. In the dojo, according to many instructors, there is no cruelty – and pain is a lesson well learned; the YMCA karate club adhered to this maxim and did its best to teach everyone a lesson, no matter who they were. On one occasion, there had been a national Wado Ryu squad training session held at the YMCA dojo and a young Japanese instructor, who had apparently won an All-Japan Universities championship, had exactly the same sort of treatment meted out to him. He had hit the floor many, many times. To his credit, he did keep hauling himself upright many, many times. The samurai had a saying of which the young Japanese champion was probably aware: '*Kikioji, mikuzure, futanren.*' *Kikioji* is being afraid of an enemy's reputation; *mikuzure* is being afraid because how the adversary looks; *futanren* is inadequate training; and any one of these three is enough to lose a fight. The reputation, grade, or the way a visitor looked, counted for nothing in the YMCA dojo and in that way, everyone was treated equally. If a visitor held his own, as only a few did, he could walk from the dojo with a real sense of achievement – and take with him the respect of the karateka with whom he had trained.

*

As I walked from the tower block where I lived, there were only signs of disrespect for people of my background. In the short time

72

since I had moved to my flat there had been a proliferation of racist graffiti and National Front stickers that were plastered over empty shopfronts and hoardings. Most of this activity was due to local council elections and as part of its campaign the NF was labelling immigrants responsible for every social ill. Unemployment, crime levels and the state of the health service were all supposedly the fault of people like my hard-working, law-abiding parents. It made me furious – and frustrated, as I had yet to see anyone actually putting up a National Front poster, or scrawl one of their slogans: like nocturnal animals, they only seemed to appear at night.

At nine o'clock on every Sunday morning Mr. Kovac, one of my neighbours who lived in the flat directly opposite mine, would make the slow and steady walk down to the newsagents in the nearby high street. He was an elderly Hungarian man who did not appear to have many friends and he always expressed his delight when I accompanied him. Often, he would have me spellbound with stories from his youth, in what he called the "old country". Occasionally, I would try to match him with colourful events that had happened in my life but they always seemed pale in comparison.

On hearing the familiar clunk of his front door, I simultaneously opened mine and he greeted me in his harsh Hungarian accent, that had never softened despite the years he had spent in England. We walked together along the murky landing and I wished bad luck on the person who had stolen yet another light-bulb from the passageway. While we waited for the lift, we made small talk about the weather. "Are you going karate chopping today?" he asked, changing the subject while making a swiping motion with his hands in gentle mockery.

"Not today, we don't start running again until next week. But that doesn't stop you coming training with me. You're not too old for me to give you a beating, you know." I replied jokingly. Mr. Kovac laughed and said he had enough trouble keeping his wife from beating him when he misbehaved. "How is your wife?" I asked, "I haven't seen her around lately."

"Her legs are playing up," Mr. Kovac replied. "They hurt sometimes. She is resting and getting her strength up for her visit to Hungary next week."

"Are you going too?" I asked.

He answered falteringly, "Hungary is my home, my beloved country, but I can't go back."

His face showed signs of great pain and I decided not to inquire about why he could not return. From our previous conversations, I knew Mr. Kovac still carried the scars of experiences from his younger days and they were matters best left untouched. "How long is your wife going for?"

"Two weeks. Her sister died recently."

The lift doors opened and I saw how dried blood speckled its walls. I took a hesitant step inside, chilled by the sight.

"It's only a little blood. It won't hurt. I saw plenty of blood as a young man. Some of it was the blood of my friends," Mr. Kovac said, as he pushed the button for the ground floor.

"What's all this?" I asked, seeing what I thought was more than "a little blood".

Mr. Kovac looked at me quizzically, and then he said, "Probably from those wild young men on the top floor. They are always cutting themselves or each other."

"You mean those skinheads?"

"Yes, those poor boys covered in all those tattoos. They are lost souls."

"I can't believe you call them 'poor boys'. I hate them," I snarled. "If they had their way, I would not even be in this country. And believe you me, you'd be on the next boat."

On hearing the anger in my voice the old man shook his head. "You don't understand what I said. They should be pitied, they are being used by others. They are not much different to you or me. Just like so many of you people, they have slipped through the cracks of society and they are often pushed to express themselves through violence. They are young, they are uneducated."

74

"These skinheads are all in the NF and want to hurt innocent people," I protested. "You know the Front was trying to organize a march the other day, just to stir up more trouble, don't you?"

I had the feeling that Mr. Kovac did not always understand me. "Don't forget most of them are ignorant of the real world," he said. "They, like so many young people, only know the little world they see and live in. And isn't England a country of free speech? Maybe it is better to let them march and vent their frustration that way."

The lift doors slid open. "But you shouldn't be free to stir up hatred with lies," I said.

"Yes, yes, I agree," said Mr. Kovac, as he moved stiffly beside me, "I've seen it all before in my country with the Jews. They felt they could not assimilate with other people because they were hated by a few, but their religious beliefs kept them separate too. This kind of separation feeds on itself, it feeds suspicion and gives one group a reason to hate the other and stay apart. And so many of them fail to recognize that we share the same humanity until it is too late."

We walked in silence for the rest of the short journey to the shop. We had our newspapers and were making our way back to the flats as I continued to try and work out if I agreed with – or even properly understood – what Mr. Kovac had said. The lights of a pelican crossing changed for us and a car pulled up; I was still figuring out how I should reply to him while we were crossing the road and did I not pay much attention to it. A blast of 'Land of Hope and Glory' from two large speaker horns on the car's roof startled me and turned my head. A call of: "ENGLAND FOR THE ENGLISH – REPATRIATE NOW!" accompanied the music.

I stopped in the road and glared at the man in the passenger seat who held the microphone handset. At first he smirked but it soon gave way to a grimace. Staring at him, I experienced a similar hatred to the one I had previously felt for the skinhead leaving the lift. But now there were no boxes in my hand to prevent me from acting. I turned and spat onto the car's bonnet. The two men in the car made nervous smiles as I trembled with anger. I made to rush to the car's door, to rip it open but a strong hand grabbed me by the shoulder and dragged me back.

The car sped off and my elderly neighbour asked, "Are you a special kind of stupid? Can you not see they are taunting you, to get you to react . . . I've seen it all before with the Nazis. . . . Nothing changes."

We reached the other side of the road as the car continued to spew its venomous message and I was not sure if I should have felt glad that Mr. Kovac had intervened to stop the situation from escalating. As if he were reading my thoughts, he said, "Don't let them upset you. You were right to move away. You could not have won. Maybe you punch them around but the courts would make sure you lose." Passers-by, who had witnessed the incident, were staring at me before hurrying on as if to avoid the gaze of a mad man. "They have to be fought in other ways," continued Mr. Kovac. "They are out because there is an election, if you really want to stop them then make sure you vote for one of the parties who oppose them." I did not have to say it, my neighbour could tell by my expression that I had not even registered to vote. He rested a hand on my shoulder and said, "But you are still young, Ralph, and one day you will find out that not even your karate will allow you to win every fight."

It would be some time before I would learn how right Mr. Kovac had been during that Sunday morning walk.

— Chapter Nine —

Without the correct principle the fight
cannot be won.
Miyamoto Musashi — The Wind Book

SCOTLAND WAS MY was my first foray to a foreign land and as we set off that morning I really did not know what to expect. The journey Clinton, Leslie and I made by train was so long and tedious that it felt as though we were travelling halfway across the globe – and several time zones – to a location that should have been a lot more exotic than Glasgow, given all our efforts to get there. Leslie could not keep still and he spent most of the time going from carriage to carriage but Clinton was a lot more laidback, he spent the hours peering out at the flickering countryside. As time went by he became less responsive and for a long while I watched how he impassively stared out of the window, as if he were completely oblivious to my presence. I wondered what was on his mind, for although I had known him most of his life, he had never been easy to read. He could do some strange things and pissing through a fence at a group of men who were armed with clubs, as he had done when we were kids, was by no means the most peculiar thing he had ever performed. But in more recent times he had withdrawn not only from me but other family members and friends, especially Leslie. At least I could always get some response from him, with a bit of effort, but there were times when he would completely ignore everyone else around him. I was about to raise the question that had been preying on my mind for some time when Leslie entered the compartment and asked if we were going to get something to eat. I was hungry and got to my feet immediately but Clinton did not respond until I touched his shoulder and asked if he were coming with us. His head turned slowly and then jerked back as if he were surprised to see me. "Coming for some food, Clint?" I asked him. He smiled weakly and muttered that he was not hungry. Leslie bad-temperedly told me to leave him to starve. He had always been low on empathy.

On finally reaching Glasgow we caught a taxi to the hotel that had been mentioned in our letters. As the driver chatted incessantly, in an accent that none of us understood, the three of us took in the sights. They did not leave us greatly impressed as the grey and overcast sky made the surroundings appear grim and forbidding. Once at the hotel, we were allocated rooms and given a sheaf of papers that included a timetable; directions to the stadium; and a list of prohibited activities. One which stuck in my mind was the rule against leaving the hotel after 5pm but the list of restrictions only served to remind me that this was no holiday excursion.

Once we had deposited our bags in our rooms we went downstairs where the Scottish karate officials gave us a welcome that contrasted with the cold and drab afternoon. We had headed north thinking of ourselves as representing the YMCA but, as the evening wore on, it was obvious that our hosts saw us as part of the people they referred to as the 'Auld Enemy'. I had been sent an England badge that was to be sewn onto the jacket of my karate gi with the letter confirming my selection but even though I had thrown mine into the rubbish bin, I was still identified as a member of an 'invading force' that the Scots told us they would take great pleasure in repelling. As a few more drinks were downed by our hosts, it became plain to me that the talk about being 'part of the enemy' was not all light-hearted banter: there was real venom behind the words. I was feeling the first stirring of a minor identity crisis: while I had been born in England, I had never considered myself, nor ever felt regarded, as English. Neither Clinton nor Leslie seemed to be troubled in the same way; to them our selection for the England under-21 team was simply a means of enhancing our competition skills and providing an opportunity to compete at European junior championships. They were confident too that the Scots would not be much opposition – but I was not so sure.

Scotland, given its small population, had always been disproportionately successful at karate. Jerome Atkinson had often talked with great respect about his Scottish team-mates in the British squad, such as the world champions Jim Collins and Pat McKay. While he had beaten Hamish Adam, who had been a member of the team that had won the world championships in 1975, to win his first European Wado Ryu title, Jerome had often mentioned how hard a fight the much smaller Scotsman had given him. And I had overheard Jerome often sing the praises of a fighter named Davy Coulter and Declan Byrne recount how the five-eight Scot had downed a German opponent, who was at least a foot taller, with one of the best techniques he had ever seen performed on a competition mat.

The following day, as we headed off to the competition venue, I stepped out of the hotel and a very large pigeon dropping splashed onto my head. It proved to be a source of great amusement for Clinton and Leslie all the way to the stadium but I was just hoping that it was not a bad omen.

As part of the standard procedure, we reported to a doctor for a very basic medical to make sure that we were fit enough to fight. My heart rate was deemed to be very slow but that was not out of the ordinary for someone so very fit. Leslie also passed with flying colours but there was a problem with Clinton. Shortly after his blood pressure was checked, he began to complain of pains in his chest and lay down on the floor. The doctor examined him but could not find anything wrong. However, after a brief consultation with the competition's officials, Clinton was told that he would not be allowed to fight and that he should get a thorough medical checkup once he was back home.

The news that Clinton was not competing unsettled me. Leslie dismissed the episode as a matter of Clinton losing his nerve but I knew that could not be the case. Physically, at least, Clinton was about as fearless as any person I had ever met, to the point he had at times displayed a reckless disregard for his own safety and like the rest of his family, he had that certain 'something' that made him a natural fighter. He was still on my mind as I prepared for my first fight. Roared on by a partisan crowd, the Scottish competitors lined up at the edge of the mat. As the subsequent bouts would prove, point-scoring was only a secondary consideration for them, the first was to dish out as much punishment to the 'Sassenachs' as the rules would allow.

Although it was not without its uncomfortable moments, I revelled in the hostile atmosphere the spectators had created and managed to win all my bouts. But that could not be said for all of my team-mates and I left the stadium with, what was for me, the rare feeling of being part of a losing side. I was also a little bruised. My first taste of international competition had been a painful reminder of how much more training I needed in my preparation for the European championships.

*

In the three weeks since our trip to Scotland, Clinton had not visited his doctor to find out the cause of his chest pains. Before he left for home an official had told him that if he were to compete at the European under-21 championships he would first have to produce a medical report giving him the all-clear. Something about my cousin had changed. Physically he seemed fine again and I started to think that perhaps Leslie had been right and Clinton had simply let the occasion get to him and he had temporarily lost his nerve. That he had not bothered with seeing his doctor might have been due to an awareness on his part that there was nothing physically wrong. Certainly, there was nothing to prevent him from returning to work obsessively on his car. The old banger still remained outside his house and despite not getting it to move an inch, he was spending what little savings he had on it. I was worried – mostly that he no longer shared my ambition to succeed in the competition arena and that the car was distracting him from getting back to our harsh training routine, much like how our cousin Errol had got distracted and never returned to the dojo once he had discovered girls and cars. Takamizawa once said that if you are finding karate easy, then you are not doing karate. Karate training is hard, unnaturally hard, and it becomes a constant battle in which the mind has to overcome the body's inclination to take the path of least resistance – the method which involves less pain and effort. Many of the karateka I knew who had finished completely with training did so after an injury, or after a summer holiday, when a week or two without training turned into a month and despite the promises to do otherwise, every passing day made returning to the rigours of the dojo that bit more difficult until it finally became impossible to return. Clinton had been told to rest for a couple of weeks, which had already turned into three and I was determined that he would be back training before it became a month.

Karate is far from being the only activity in which one has to overcome the instinct to avoid pain; for example, long distance runners have to confront their bodies' aversion to being tested to the limits over many miles in all sorts of weather and conditions. I thought it no coincidence that the greatest karate competitor I knew, Jerome Atkinson, had also run a number of marathons. Karate and marathon running have a lot in common as it is as much about the condition of the mind as it is of the body and I thought the best way to get Clinton training again was to get him to run with me.

He had spoken no more than a few words since we began running from his house. He was such a good athlete that, if he wanted, he could talk effortlessly while running but as we headed through the prosperous suburbs his grim silence again turned my mind to what was going on inside his head. Perhaps his quietness was an easy companionable sort, or it was an indicator of his determination to succeed. Or maybe it was another indicator of something more dire: I had a feeling about what was wrong with Clinton but it was so awful that I spent a lot of my time convincing myself that I was wrong, especially every time the cousin I knew reappeared. However, the Clinton I had known since we were both small kids seemed to exist for periods that were getting shorter and shorter. As I had done during our train journey to Scotland, I wanted to ask him about his state of mind but I did not know how to broach the subject without offending him. The incident in Glasgow continued to concern me but every time I wavered, my doubts and fears were pushed back further into a recess in my mind and made them much harder to voice.

Clinton began to accelerate and made it clear that my overall physical fitness needed to be taken to a higher level. It was the one weak link in my preparation. Weight training had left me stronger than I had ever been and I had learnt during the fights with the Scottish competitors that if I wanted to succeed at international level, it was necessary to concentrate on improving my techniques by way of even more hours of constant repetition. Running the six-mile course was the first step in a programme I had devised to increase my stamina.

My pace quickened to match Clinton's. He responded in kind. Now our arms and legs were pumping furiously and for a few fleeting seconds we were rapt in the exuberance of our own physicality – until I suddenly realized the gate that kept the beast of number 52 at bay had been left open. Our feet thundered on the concrete; we were going too fast to stop. Every time we had run past number 52 the German Shepard had attacked the gate while barking viciously. Someone at the dojo knew of a white man who had trained his dog to attack only black people but it was not until the day a blonde pear-shaped woman in a primrose jog suit had ambled on ahead of us without drawing so much as a yap that it occurred to me that the brute *did* reserve its performance for only black passers-by. Or maybe it simply smelled my fear. Before I had time to come to a conclusion, it was upon us. Finding a speed I never knew I possessed, I left Clinton behind but the German Shepard chose to stay on my heels. I was across the road and without a second's hesitation, or looking for the traffic, I scrambled onto the bonnet of a parked car. As the gnashing teeth closed in, I climbed onto its roof.

Seeking easier prey, the dog turned its attention to Clinton. But he was putting what I later described as "my diversionary tactic" to good use by ripping a wooden fencing pole from a front garden. Instead of running away, Clinton screamed while he raced towards our four-legged tormentor with the piece of wood raised above his head. The large mutt seemed momentarily unsure of what to make of the approaching phenomenon and then turned tail as the pole made contact with its backside. With a mixture of relief and annoyance, I screamed curses at the dog and its owners as it fled back to the sanctuary of its own yard. Dropping the fencing pole, and without a second glance at me perched on top the car, Clinton continued with his run.

Before the dog had a chance to rediscover its courage, or the owner of the car caught sight of me and the damage I had caused, I scampered off the deeply dented roof and sprinted to catch up with Clinton. It took some distance before I reached him and as I drew level he stopped suddenly.

"What's up, Clint?" I asked, as he folded and gripped his knees. His whole body was shaking and I immediately thought he was having some sort of seizure. It was only as he straightened that I realized that it was laughter that had sent him into convulsions.

Gasping for air, he said, "Do you remember when Leslie fought that one-legged man?"

It was an incident at a tournament in the north of England that all those who had watched it could hardly forget. Leslie had been drawn against a young man who had an artificial leg and the referee had approached Leslie before the contest to ask if he would make it more of an exhibition bout as the youth had entered the competition as more of a gesture about overcoming a disability rather than with any real notion of winning. Leslie nodded but when the bout began he made it into an exhibition of his ruthlessness. Within seconds he had swept the artificial leg from beneath the youth and followed up with a punch as his opponent lay spreadeagled on the mat. He did this not once but twice, to the horror of his instructor, his team-mates and the spectators, and he was duly awarded the fight. When I later asked him why he had been so cruelly efficient he replied, "He wanted to be treated just like any other person, didn't he? So, I treated the guy like everyone else. And besides, I wasn't going to take any chance of losing to no one-foot boy because I took it easy."

"But, Les," I began to protest.

Leslie was having none of it. "Ralph, karate isn't easy," he said. "Life isn't easy and a guy with only one leg should know that already."

And they say there is no cruelty in karate.

Clinton was still laughing as I finally answered his question and told him that I could never forget what Leslie had done that day. "Well," he laughed, "I was thinking that dog almost made you into another one-footed fighter and what Les would've made of it."

We continued with our run and I grunted a few things about the possibility of racist dogs but he did not respond. Within a matter of yards he had withdrawn again behind an impassive expression and as we returned to our starting point he ran into his house without a word of farewell. I thought about following him inside. I hovered for a few moments trying to work out what I would say to Clinton about his behaviour but the sweat was already growing cold upon my skin and I retreated to my car. Reluctantly, I turned the ignition: whatever there was to say to Clinton would have to wait for another day.

— Chapter Ten —

*Make your body like a rock and ten
thousand things cannot touch you.
Miyamoto Musashi — The Fire Book*

FOUR DAYS AFTER my run with Clinton, Mr. Kovac my
Hungarian neighbour met me at the front door of my flat. He
looked down to the floor and saw that I too had been posted
National Front leaflets, even though the local elections had long
gone. He told me that everyone on our floor had received one
and that I had not been singled out. I told him that I did not even
bother to pick them up, never mind read them: they would go out
with the trash. Almost apologetically, he added my dad had called
around and asked him to pass on the message that a relative of
mine had been admitted to the hospital with pains in his chest
and head. I immediately knew who it was.

At least a dozen family members were at the hospital by the
time I got there. After a few hours of hearing no news on Clinton's
condition, some of them left saying they would return later and
asked those of us who remained to telephone them should there
be any developments. I passed the time at the vending machine
and chatted to a few of the nurses. I had been in the Accident and
Emergency Unit so often, either as a patient or accompanying a
fellow karateka who had been injured in the dojo, that I was on
first name terms with quite a few of them.

A grim-faced doctor finally emerged from behind a curtain and announced that we could all go home. He said that Clinton was feeling a lot better and although no evidence of any *physical* ailment could be found, he would be kept in overnight for observation. The news was received with a collective sigh of relief from the family but I knew that every one of us secretly shared a suspicion about what was wrong. Most took the easy way out by accepting the doctor's words but I remained sceptical. I had heard the way he had used the word 'physical' and I had seen it all before in Scotland. Like the doctor, I felt that Clinton's condition was due to something more than a *physical* illness.

While some of the family made phone calls, the rest chose to linger and create a jubilant atmosphere which was totally out of sorts with the disinfected surroundings. Clinton was being cared for in a small cubical that had curtains at each end and I waited for a nurse to step out before sneaking in to find him lying on a bed. He was perfectly still and appeared to be sleeping. Quietly sitting beside him, I held his hand as I saw the streaks that had been left by the tears than had run down his cheeks. His eyes opened and he greeted me with a smile. "Feeling any better?" I asked.

He squeezed my hand. "Yeah," he said softly.

I felt my lip tremble. "What's the matter, Clint?" I asked. "You had us all worried again with those chest pains."

"I don't know exactly . . . Sometimes my chest hurts . . . Mainly it's my head . . . I sometimes get confused." His fingers tightened around mine. "Hey, Ralph, I'm frightened. I just want to go home."

"Do you mind?" boomed a voice from behind me. "You will have to leave. All of you. Those outside as well, you will have to go home. There's nothing you can do here."

I was led out of the cubicle by the ward sister, who then herded me with the rest of the family toward the exit. From behind the curtain Clinton laughed. Despite my worries, my heart was warmed by the happy sound from inside the cubicle. Clinton's laughter continued to cut through the sterile air as I made my way outside but that the laughter was so prolonged made me grit my teeth and I went home feeling scared for my cousin Clinton.

*

It looked like events had conspired to disrupt my preparations for the European under-21 championships. Although my overall physical condition remained good, I had received stitches above my eye courtesy of a punch during a particularly hard training session. Eddie Cox had told the class to divide into three groups of ten karateka, one of whom would stand ready in a fighting stance against a wall while the other nine made a line and took turns to attack to him. There could be no retreat, only movement to the side, or forward to meet the attack. When nine attacks were completed, the person at the front of the line would take his place against the wall. We would go round and round, sometimes having to act as the defender four or five times. It was an exhausting exercise for the defender, who was not allowed to rest, while those who were attacking were not only resting as they waited for their turn but they were also scrutinizing the defender's tactics and then plotting a means to catch him out as they made their way to the front of the line. It was almost impossible not to take at least one hard blow during this exercise and Trog took full advantage of me trying to regain my wind after taking a powerful kick to the stomach from Clinton, of all people. It had been a couple of weeks since his scare and although he had been given a clean bill of health and was back training I was saddened, but not surprised, when he told me that he would not be coming with me to the European championships in London. I had got hit by two consecutive attacks – Clinton's kick and Trog's punch – but I still had to defend myself against another four before the change came and I went to the back of the line. The sight of my blood seemed to spur on the karateka in front of me. Their punches and kicks came faster and harder as they tried to take advantage of my weakened state. But I did not take it personally, they were only doing what they were trained to do.

*

87

At Crystal Palace I reported to Doctor Canning, the medical officer for the British team, still fretting that the cut over my eye would stop me from fighting. The stitches were still in place but the skin was healing and he said that I would be okay to compete. "A word of advice, Ralph," he said as I left him, "just don't get punched there again."

The championships were to be held over two days and I stayed at one of the hotels close to Crystal Palace with other members of the squad. One of them was a black guy from the Afan Lido club in Wales named Bird; he had also been selected to fight in the heavy-weight category. Despite the trouble we both had in understanding each other's accents, we had struck up a rapport. Bird was fast and had a great range of techniques but I had fought him in the past and thought I could beat him again if the gold medal were at stake. He was also tall but it was not until I faced my first opponent that I realized that his height was not exceptional in the heavyweight division. But I was not intimidated; I stepped out onto the mat for that first fight almost bursting with pent-up aggression.

I returned to the hotel satisfied with my efforts after the first day of competition, not only had I (along with my roommate) reached the semifinal stage of the individual tournament but so had the team of which both of us were members. The disparity in size had not counted against me and my aggression and my ability to anticipate my opponents' attacks had enabled me to comfort-ably win all my bouts. As I retired to my bed, Bird said, "You fought good today."

I said, "Well, Birdie, I saw you fight. You were brilliant." He laughed in acknowledgment of my recognition of his attempt at a good-humoured mind-game. We had watched each other's progress with interest and had figured that there was a strong possibility that we would face each other in the heavyweight final.

Once the lights were off, I began to imagine what glory the following day might have in store for me. A change of tactics would be needed – aggression would not be enough – if I were to progress to the final. The other three fighters who remained in my category all looked capable of winning a gold medal – and, more importantly, had seen the way I fought.

The second day of the championships progressed quickly and it did not seem long before I was called to the mat for the semifinal. My prize was now tantalizingly close: two more fights and the title of European under-21 Heavyweight champion would be mine. Bird and I were to face two Italian fighters, the tall Guazzaroni brothers. Both of them would become top class competitors and one would win a world championship seven years later. My fight would be the first of the two semifinals and I thought it was a blessing as it gave me less time to be nervous.

When the fight got under way, I found that my cagey Italian opponent anticipated my movements extremely well. He had obviously watched me fight and figured a way to counter my style. His offence, on the other hand, had me baffled. Attacks were launched from unorthodox stances and almost caught me off guard. On several occasions I just managed to evade his punches and kicks and the fear of losing a fight entered my head for the first time: it would prove to be a costly lapse in concentration. We continued to shuffle around the mat and I was thinking about what tactic I should employ next when a lightening-fast uraken strike with his front hand slammed against the side of my forehead, close to my cut. My eyes smarted as the referee inspected my injury for any further damage before he gestured toward my opponent and awarded him a half-point.

He was gaining in confidence and looked to quickly capitalize on his advantage with another attack. I did not see it coming but instinctively I moved my head and the bottom of his heel scraped the other side of my face as he attempted to hit me with an axe kick. To add to my indignity, the judge's arm shot up to award an *ippon* but he was overruled by the referee after he had halted the bout for a brief consultation. Now I was livid. "Screw the tactics," I growled under my breath. I had got this far by fighting to my strengths but now I was thinking too much about tactics. After all, in Japanese martial arts, the practitioner strives for *mushin* – no mind – when in a combat situation so as the body can react without the conscious thoughts that make the actions too ponderous to be effective. In that instant I decided to revert to the aggressive use of the techniques that had been honed in the YMCA dojo. The referee called for the fight to restart as I thought how I would make my opponent pay for trying to embarrass me.

I threw a feint. He reacted. I smiled to myself, now I had him. Another feint and he pulled away slightly. The first two punches of my combination only met thin air but the third landed on his chest with a thud. "*Wazari!*"called the referee. I had found his weakness and no sooner had I been awarded the half-point that I was back at him. The stinging pain above my eye dictated my next move. Mimicking his technique, I hit him to the side of his face using uraken and immediately followed it up with another powerful reverse punch to his chest – "*Ippon!*"

I did not allow him to settle after that and continued to force him back until the referee brought the fight to an end with a call of "*Yame!*"

The national team coach congratulated me as I left the mat but my satisfaction with winning the bout was short-lived, as he reminded me that I had to maintain my focus for one more fight. Relaxing between fights was something I did naturally, I'd even been known to fall asleep, but as I waited for the final I continually walked anxiously around the arena. Some team members offered words of encouragement as I walked by but their words fell on deaf ears. It was then that I missed the support of my fellow members of the YMCA club. Most of all I missed Clinton's presence.

After what seemed an interminable wait, it was announced that the final was about to get underway. My heartbeat quickened. I approached the mat and paced the perimeter of the fighting area, trying not to look across to my opponent. I was to fight the second Italian for the title as, to my surprise, he had convincingly beaten Bird. He too was pacing the floor despite his trainer beckoning for him to sit down and relax. The British coach said something to me that I could not make out as I exhaled heavily through rapidly drying lips. I walked toward my line. After bowing to the referee I faced my opponent. His bow toward me was far more gracious than the perfunctory nod I gave him. My legs and arms started to tingle as the referee took a step back. He motioned with his two hands and I felt a bead of sweat trickle down the hollow of my back. My calves tightened as I readied myself to spring from the line and with a shout of "*Hajime!*" he signalled for the bout to begin.

The fight started with furious exchanges. We shared a similar aggressive style of fighting. He scored first with a punch, gyakuzuki; I equalized shortly after with a maegeri that drove the air out of him. He quickly recovered his wind and scored again with another punch to the body, I did likewise. He changed stance and fought with his right foot forward, his hands constantly moving. I attacked and another punch landed on my body, high up near my shoulder but it was still adjudged to have scored. He tried to press home his advantage and attacked with a high kick. I sidestepped but he had moved out of reach by the time I threw a counterattack that brushed his gi. He bounced around on the balls of his feet, still moving his hands in a threatening way, but he made no attempt to attack. He was playing for time, time that was rushing by for me now I was behind in the scoring. I moved forward throwing punches to head and body. He swayed and parried. My ashi barai swept his front leg away and had him tumbling to the mat but I failed to follow up with a clean scoring technique. Back on my line, the muscles in my legs were coiled to push me forward for one last attempt to score when the bell sounded. The referee shouted that the bout was at an end before he turned to check the score. He then moved back to his line and stood with his hands at his side. For moments of aching intensity, I willed that the score was not how I had counted it and that his right hand would shoot out in my direction, or at least signal a draw. But it was his left hand that was raised after he had announced that my opponent had won by three *wazaris* to two.

My insides felt as though they had collapsed with the weight of disappointment. The customary handshake at the end of the bout was dispensed with as my opponent rushed over and hugged me. He was ecstatic but I just stood there with my arms limply at my side, hardly believing that I had been beaten. It felt as though I had briefly held the gold medal in my palm only for someone else to snatch it away before my fingers could curl around it.

Losing was something I had never considered during all my long and tortuous preparations for the competition and although the notion had briefly entered my head in the semifinal I had banished the thought from my mind and had managed to win. I took my example from Jerome Atkinson, who while a very modest man, had complete faith in his own ability and it always came as a surprise to him when, on very rare occasions, he lost. Deflated and frustrated, I had to compose myself as I would be competing in a short while in the team event. The British under-21 team bristled with raw talent and such was our level of performance during the qualification rounds that I could not see any other team preventing us from winning the gold medal, which would be of some small consolation to me. But for some reason the team coach changed the lineup that had previously done so well and inserted fighters from his own club. Not only were the new fighters not as good as those they had replaced, it was a move that undermined the spirit of those of us who remained. Although I won my fight, the team lost its semifinal and was only good enough for a third place and a bronze medal. My frustration was turning into anger and I went and took myself away from my fellow squad members so I could be alone with my thoughts.

I had been sitting morosely with a towel over my head replaying the only fight I had lost in two days of competition when an official with the British squad told me to put on my tracksuit for the medal ceremony. Without uncovering my head, I told him that I did not have a tracksuit. "Ralph, it's part of the dress code," he said, by way of explaining why he was still standing over me.

"I never got a tracksuit," I said.

"And you never got a badge to sew onto your gi either?"

He was referring to the small embroidered representation of the Union Jack that I had thrown into a bin, as I had done with the England badge, before the match with Scotland. My reluctance to display a national allegiance had obviously been noted. "It's on my other gi," I replied, "I brought this one by mistake. Don't worry about the tracksuit, a lot of the fighters from other countries don't have one."

"It's *our* code," he insisted. "No tracksuit, no medal."

"That's okay with me," I said.

From under the edge of my towel I saw him flounce away in his grey flannels and navy jacket, which had a badge on its breast pocket that proudly proclaimed his allegiance to Britain, or at least to her karate team. I imagined that whoever he was talking to would put my truculence down to the bitter disappointment of losing in the final but the shrewder amongst them would read something else into my motives. I saw the flannels and a tracksuit approach. I lifted the towel to see the team coach with a tracksuit top in his hand. "Use this one for the ceremony, eh, Ralph?" he said, as he thrust it toward me. I gazed at its little embroidered flag and there was a moment in which I paused and thought about handing back the tracksuit. It was the same emblem I had seen on the car that had carried around men from the National Front, it was the flag that appeared on the literature they had pushed through my door; it had become a symbol of hate and the sight of it turned my stomach. When that moment had passed I guessed my gesture of refusing my medals would be lost on most of the people gathered in Crystal Palace and it would be characterized as the action of a sore loser. After a heavy sigh I put on the tracksuit top and made my way to the podium.

Watching the Italian flag being raised above the Union Jack filled me with a cocktail of conflicting emotions. It was only then that it truly hit home that I had lost. But at the same time I was glad that there was not about to be a rendition of 'God Save the Queen' because of my efforts. After another hug from the affectionate victor, I stepped down from the platform before another embrace provoked me into doing something that could set off an international incident. By the time my foot touched the floor I was already taking off the tracksuit top and within moments it was back with the coach. I knew he did not understand that what he had asked me to wear was like adding an insult to my injured feelings.

— Chapter Eleven —

*You must thoroughly cut down the enemy so
that he does not recover his position.
Miyamoto Musashi — The Fire Book*

THE NEWS OF my European silver medal drew copious congrat-
ulations from Mick Davies at the factory. His reaction was in sharp
contrast to those I had encountered back at the dojo. My team-
mates found it hard to be so effusive because they knew how disappointed I was with second place. The one exception was Trog, as
usual, he had plenty to say. He grinned broadly as he 'congratulated' me on making it to the final. "Getting beat when you were
so close must've been hard to take, eh?" he chuckled. But Mick
could only see my medal as a great achievement and urged me
to announce the result to the rest of the factory by way of display-
ing my medal in the canteen. Perhaps he was trying to make
amends for the indifference displayed by the other guys seated
at the long table in the maintenance department.

"Go on," Mick said, as we headed to the stamp shop.

"Go on what?"

"Go on and bring in your medal. Before you say no, a bloke in
the machine shop is always bringing in his fishing trophies and the
darts team is always sticking newspaper cuttings on the notice board.
Go on, Ralph, lots of people would like to see it. You must be the
first person from the factory ever to represent Britain in anything."

Maybe he was appealing to a vanity I denied possessing but for the first time I began to consider bringing my medal to work; that was until we reached the machine we were to repair. Four men were standing around drawing on scrawny roll-up cigarettes as they waited for us. Mick dropped his toolbox and to the oldest one he said, "Bert, I was just saying Ralph must be the first bloke in the factory to ever represent Great Britain in any sport."

Bert, a fat man with a silver Teddy-boy quiff, blew smoke from the side of his mouth. I had always been aware of a certain malevolence in his eyes but it was something to which Mick remained completely oblivious. "Oh yes?" Bert said. "What sport, exactly?"

Embarrassed, I bent down and pretended to be looking in my tool box as Mick replied, "He was fighting for the British karate team at the European championships at the weekend – and won a silver medal." I was wishing Mick had kept quiet as I straightened up. There was a scornful twist on Bert's lip as he said, "Fighting for Britain. Well, there's a thing." He turned to the others and said, "Did you know he was fighting for Britain?"

"I thought he'd be fighting for Jamaica or some other African country," one laughed.

"You daft bastard," I growled, "it was the European championships. In case you didn't know, Jamaica's a Caribbean country . . . A long, long way from Europe."

I hunkered down next to Mick and began to work on the machine but the response I waited for never came. I thought someone might say: "Never mind where Jamaica is, you couldn't pass for an Englishman." There had been a few snide comments after I had fought for England in the match against Scotland, stuff like: "I didn't realize you qualified for England, Ralph," or "Nice to hear you were defending our English heritage for us against those bloody Jocks." It was those sorts of comments which had made it so difficult for me to put on that tracksuit top before the medal ceremony.

Mick had heard the comments too and told me to take no notice of them. It was not as easy as that for me. At some point during my life the concept that I was an outsider had crept into my consciousness and I did not know if the idea were mine, or if it were a reflection of how I was perceived by others. The local National Front was doing its level best to foment conflict by continually handing out provocative literature around where I lived and had me retreating behind some kind of mental barricade. Similar stuff had got put up at work but it was quickly taken down by the management who made it clear that any employee who was found in possession of such inflammatory racist material would be instantly dismissed. I straightened up once the repair was finished and each of the four men looked at me in a manner that made me wonder which one of them had put up a National Front poster in the washroom.

It should not have affected me but the reaction of Bert and his three mates had got under my skin and the prospect of another forty-five years of work was starting to get me down. If karate had provided me with many of the highs, every day I spent at the factory was beginning to feel like a low. I sought comfort in the notion that I had only a few months of my apprenticeship remaining and, provided I passed my exams at night school, I would then be fully qualified – and free to move on.

Perhaps losing in the final had been no big catastrophe in the great scheme of things but it was a straw of misery that had threatened to make the load I felt on my young shoulders much harder to bear. Questions about Clinton's state of health remained on my mind; work was doing its best to suck any vitality from me; and returning to an empty flat did nothing to lighten my mood. Before the European championships I had called on my childhood sweetheart in an attempt to break the monotony of my solitary lifestyle. Hilda was very pretty, intelligent and the object of desire for many guys I knew. We had originally split up because her mother had gone out of her way to make things very difficult for us. But seeing Hilda again had only increased the feeling of loneliness and had not diminished it.

It was a Friday evening when I thought about contacting her

again but there was a beauty contest at the Rising Star and I did not think Hilda would appreciate a night out with me as I ogled a score of local women in swimsuits. I slapped on some aftershave and thought I would see if I could rekindle our relationship just a little more – but not on a 'boys night out'. Hilda could wait for another night.

*

The club was packed out and I was doing my best to find a better view of the stage when a tap on my shoulder turned me around. It was Ewart. He had a look on his face that communicated that there was trouble afoot and with a nod of his head he indicated for me to follow him outside. I expected that there was a gang of rowdy young men who were unwilling to accept that the club was full but except for Jerome and a couple of regular customers the foyer was empty. Ewart told Jerome he would see him in a while and went outside. Pete, a karateka who had remained a green belt since the day I began training, was waiting for us in his car. Ewart got in next to Pete and with a pair of eyes that were blazing with anger, he signalled that I was to get into the back.

I still had not closed the door as the car shot off down the road. I had yet to find out what this was all about but I knew that violence was imminent. As we sped towards another nightclub, Pete gave a brief outline of what had happened. Vernon, who was still at school and the baby of the Campbell family, had persuaded Ewart to get him a job as a glass collector that would provide him with a little pocket money during the weekends. Unbeknown to Vernon, a notorious gang of thugs were in the club that night and looking for trouble. The gang was made up of black and white guys but nothing positive came out of this alliance, rather they became a feared 'crew' of football hooligans whose chief claim to notoriety came about after one of their number had stabbed a man to death in the town centre. Vernon had lifted a glass from their table he thought was 'dead' but, high on drugs and belligerence, one of the gang had snatched the glass from Vernon's hand and then thrust it at his head.

Pete's car screeched to a halt right outside the club's entrance and brought a doorman out to wave us to the far end of the car park. As soon as he saw who was in the car he backed off, Ewart also worked at this club and all the bouncers had seen him in action: they knew better than to try and stop him while he was in this mood. Ewart ignored the outstretched hand of Earl, a large doorman, as he entered the foyer. Earl knew why we were there and began giving his version of what had gone on. With a finger jabbing at a very large chest, Ewart responded by chastising Earl and the rest of the doormen: if they had been doing their job properly the gang would not have been allowed entry in the first place. Earl replied that they had ejected the gang and then got Vernon to the hospital. "Ejected?" snarled Ewart. "After what they did to my brother, he's the only one who ends up in hospital?" He did not have to say what would have been meted out if he had been there. 'Glassing' was a terrible crime that often led to permanent disfigurement but it was frequently treated with undue leniency by the legal system: the police rarely visited the crime scene and if a case did get to the courts the perpetrator often escaped with a few months in jail while the victim suffered the consequences for the rest of his, or her, life. "I want names!" Ewart demanded.

Sheepishly, Earl pointed to a group of men and women standing in the car park. "That's some of them," he said. Ewart frowned bad-temperedly, as if to ask everyone present that if they were some of the guys who were responsible for attacking Vernon, then why was it they were still conscious?

I went out with Ewart and Pete into the car park. The tallest of the group was a black man who was pulling on a cigarette as he briefly looked over to us as we approached. They were chatting amongst themselves and seemed so unconcerned that I did wonder if they could have been the ones who were responsible for attacking Vernon. Ewart beckoned to the tall man who sauntered over to us. "What?" he sneered. It was obvious that no one around the place intimidated this man, he gave off an air as if he thought of himself as untouchable. Perhaps he figured that as a member of the town's most dangerous gang he had the safety that was afforded by its reputation.

Ewart said, "I want the names and addresses of those who did the glassing."

The man put a piece of gum into his mouth and let out a disdainful chuckle as he started to chew. I thought then that he was making a very big mistake – it was not as though he had been given a right to silence in this regard. Ewart struck the man's throat with a technique called toho, which uses the hollow between the forefinger and thumb, before his fingers took hold of the throat while he simultaneously performed ashi barai to sweep away the man's legs from under him, this was followed by a stamping kick to the chest. There was a terrible beauty about Ewart's technique that I could not help but admire: he had employed exquisitely controlled techniques that were hard enough to bring down the man but not so hard as to knock him unconscious. "I want the names and addresses of those who did the glassing," Ewart repeated.

Gang members had a rule that they did not squeal – on one another – and that was how they had got away with so many crimes. Maybe it was down to a primal instinct but every one of them knew that their notion of strength had its origins in a misguided unity and without it they had nothing. The man put his health in grave danger when he refused to answer Ewart's question. He was about to take a vicious blow when a young woman screamed that she would tell Ewart what he wanted to know. She managed to stammer one name and address; there was more than one involved – but one name would be enough, for now. Ewart hauled her boyfriend upright and then threw him over the roof of a parked taxi. There was a terrible cracking noise as the man landed out of our line of vision but Ewart did not seem concerned as we headed back to Pete's car.

We got to the Campbell household shortly after Vernon had arrived there from the hospital. His head was swathed in bandages but thankfully the lacerations were away from his face. His reflexes had saved him from facial disfigurement and the glass had struck him to the side and rear of his head. He filled us in with what had happened and although he had escaped with relatively minor injuries, Ewart was still bent on vengeance. In response to his older brother's question, Vernon said that he was fit enough to travel and that he would accompany us to the address the woman had provided.

Pete and I were peering though a hedge as Ewart and Vernon went to the front porch door. A heavyset youth with tattoos on his arms, and dressed in only his boxer shorts, opened the front door but he was streetwise enough to keep the porch door only slightly ajar. He was cocky too – as he knew that there was little chance of Vernon and Ewart pulling the door open before he locked it again. I could hear Vernon verify that he was one of his attackers and the tattooed man respond that the two of them had better leave his premises or there would be "consequences". Suddenly, a middle-aged woman appeared at the man's rear; she was drunk and screaming that she did not want her son bringing trouble to her house again before slamming the front door shut behind him. Now he was trapped inside the porch. Even from where I was standing, the terror on his face was obvious. Vernon took advantage of his momentary lapse and yanked the door open before he punched the man squarely in the mouth.

It was truly amazing what fear was enabling this man to do: within an instant he had recovered from Vernon's punch and barged past him and Ewart before vaulting over a hedge that was at least five feet high. Pete and I moved to cut him off as he hurdled over picket fences that were a mere three feet tall. He was moving with the speed and grace of an Olympic hurdler until he saw that we were about to cut off his escape route. The tattooed man pivoted and started to go back over the fences he had just cleared – only to run into Ewart. The gyakuzuki was technically brilliant: it had speed; weight transfer; his rear foot, hips and shoulders had all turned in unison. The man was rendered unconscious the moment Ewart's knuckles connected with his chin and as he flew backwards through the air – and through a bay window – he was blissfully unaware that he had just been taken out with a masterful technique.

All around, lights were being switched on as we drove away and it did cross my mind what the inhabitants of the house with the broken window would have to say as they found an almost naked man lying senseless on their livingroom carpet.

I did not fully appreciate then just what I was being drawn into. Blood, in this case my cousin Vernon's blood, had been spilt and I did not give my subsequent conduct a moment's second thought. In the following weeks, despite several of them going into hiding, every gang member, whether they had been present in the club during the attack on Vernon or not, was found and dealt with – and I felt every action taken against these men was entirely justified. Years later, I read an interview with one of the country's most notorious football hooligans in a British national newspaper. It turned out he was the leader of the gang who had glassed Vernon. In proclaiming his toughness he omitted to tell the journalist of the time when he had been finally found by Ewart, how he had cried and begged for mercy – and how he consequently spent a lengthy period in a hospital. I thought then that the reputations of men such as these were piled high by people who were easily impressed, or intimidated.

— Chapter Twelve —

To all ways there are sidetracks.
Miyamoto Musashi — The Ground Book

THE ATTACK ON Vernon and its aftermath had some unexpected results: my cousin Clinton was back to his old self. It was if he had never been away. In taking part in the tracking down of his brother's attackers and then delivering the beatings that were deemed appropriate, Clinton seemed to forget about his own troubles. He also, thankfully, seemed to forget about that old wreck he had bought and now the evenings were drawing in, he was once again back to training in the dojo at every opportunity. I was now content that his health scare had been only a temporary aberration.

In a bizarre role reversal, I was the one who was falling into contemplative silences and he was asking me what was on my mind. We were in the changing room next to the dojo when Clinton asked me again about what was wrong. I had been struggling to tie my belt, which was something I had managed to do correctly for five years without too much trouble, when I took a deep breath and said, "Hilda. She's having a baby. Make that, she's having our baby."

Clinton's face lit up and he shook my hand vigorously. "And there were rumours that you weren't up to it," he laughed.

I did my best to join in with him but the laughter died in my throat. Hilda had called to my parents' house after I had failed to respond to the calls she had made to the factory – and they had guessed the nature of the news she had for me. They both liked Hilda very much and thought she was a stabilizing influence on me and my dad had made it plain that he hoped that once I became a father I would stop my karate training and live up to my responsibilities. When I met up with Hilda again, I was still unsure about how I should react to her news. I was barely twenty years old and had just made up my mind to finish working at the factory so I could do some travelling. I had fantasized about going to Japan and training at all the top dojos and then perhaps heading to Hong Kong and finding work in a few kung fu films. They were only daydreams to get me through the day at the factory but Hilda's pregnancy had robbed me of even those harmless flights of fancy. There were big, life-changing choices ahead of me and I needed more time before I came to a decision.

The talk amongst the students before the lesson began was of the final installment of retribution that had been handed out by Ewart to the leader of the football hooligan crew. When Ewart had finally found him, he suggested that they go for a drive. Away from the glare of his comrades, the so-called hard man disintegrated into a flood of tears as he was driven out to a secluded wood; Ewart did not want the screams to be heard and risk having the terrible lesson he was about to dispense being disturbed.

As we lined up for the bow, Eddie Cox scrutinized all those who made up the front row. He did not seem happy and I got the feeling that he wanted the extracurricular activities to end. He was initially sympathetic and was prepared to tolerate the odd incident but what had occurred over the previous month had been a sustained litany of very public beatings – often in someone's front garden – involving members of the YMCA karate club. During the ensuing two hours he and Declan Byrne had us practising basic techniques and kata and made it clear throughout the lesson that we were not up to scratch.

With so many tournaments around the country – and invitations for members to attend British international squad training

– there was a danger that the training in the dojo was becoming too competition-orientated. While both instructors had been successful as students, they had retired from competition karate at relatively young ages because they were not prepared to sacrifice what they considered the true essence of karate in return for success on the competition mat. In competition karate only a small percentage of a vast range of techniques is used and the most dangerous – and most effective – are banned but in Wado Ryu that percentage is even smaller because it is a fusion of Okinawan karate and Japanese jujitsu, the locks and throws of which are totally forbidden in karate contests.

Before the final bow, Cox sensei announced that there was to be a grading in a little more than three weeks time for the brown belts. Because of the regulations of Wado Ryu's governing body, examinations of grades above fourth kyu had to be taken with a Japanese instructor and so the brown belt gradings usually took place in the dojos of either Kuniaki Sakagami or Peter Suzuki – and I knew which one of the Japanese senseis everyone in the front row would have preferred. Mick Bryan could not restrain his curiosity. "Where is the grading going to be, sensei?" he asked – on everybody's behalf. A smirk twisted the lips of Eddie Cox. "At Peter Suzuki's," he said, prompting an audible hiss of displeasure to escape from us.

*

On a rainy Saturday morning I drove to Peter Suzuki's dojo in Birmingham with Clinton. The other karateka who were eligible to take a grading examination had decided to opt out and wait for a later opportunity with Sakagami sensei. Sakagami was considered far more amiable and consistent than the mercurial Peter Suzuki. While the personalities of the Japanese instructors were factors for some, for others it was down to the lack of available time in which they had to rearrange their priorities as regards their training regimes. Clinton and I agreed that the change in our routines had done us good. As with all constant repetition,

105

there is the inherent danger that you may continually reproduce the same mistakes but the practising of a range of *kihon* and *renraku waza* (basic and combination techniques) and kata had made us more aware of how our bodies were moving as we executed techniques that we had neglected over the months.

As karate emerged from the 1970s, the tension between being a traditional karateka and a competitor had grown. I had read in one of Mick's magazines that Billy Higgins, a Shotokan instructor who had come second in the 1972 world championships, reckoned that you could be a good karateka and not be a good competitor – but you could not be a good competitor without first being a good karateka. But as competition rules changed and it gradually became more about speed and touching an opponent rather than hitting him with a controlled strike, I was starting to understand Eddie Cox's view that the sporting side of karate was growing ever less relevant as a measure of how good a fighter you actually were.

The woman at the desk on the ground floor of Peter Suzuki's dojo took our grading fees and our licences – which were merely a record of our grades and not a means of registering lethal hands with the police, as commonly believed – before Clinton and I climbed the short flight of stairs to the changing room. The dojo was up yet more stairs and I entered it with a little apprehension.

I could not think of any karate student who actually liked Peter Suzuki; mostly he was feared and loathed in equal measure. He was a tall man for a Japanese and pudgy with it but it was his unpredictable character that had made him less than popular with a lot of the black belts in the area. The exception being Eddie Cox. Peter Suzuki also liked Eddie, ever since that first time he had knocked him unconscious in Sakagami's dojo. Eddie was only a green belt at the time but already had a reputation for being a better fighter than any of the black belts. Suzuki had travelled from his school in Ireland and had watched Eddie train before saying that they would spar together. This was a great compliment but it put Eddie in something of a dilemma: Peter Suzuki, as with most Japanese instructors, hated displays of cowardice – or lack of spirit as they called it – and if Eddie held back during the sparring his restraint could be interpreted as an absence of courage. However, if he went in hard this would almost certainly provoke a response that would result in the student being put firmly back into his rightful place. Eddie Cox decided that he might as well go in hard and at least emerge with some honour. The green belt more than held his own against the fifth dan black belt until Peter Suzuki called '*Yame!*' Eddie promptly halted only to knocked out cold by a technique that he never saw coming. When he was brought around, Peter Suzuki laughed and gave him a lecture about *zanshin* and always remaining aware of an opponent, no matter what. Later that year Suzuki moved to Birmingham and started to teach at the Temple Karate Centre alongside Toru Takamizawa. Eugene Codrington, another world championship runner-up and twice European heavyweight champion was a student there and undoubtedly the best competitor. He was the favourite of the slightly built and nimble Takamizawa; but for Peter Suzuki, the burly brawler, Eddie Cox was the number one student. As far as an attitude to combat went, they were kindred spirits and when Eddie was awarded his first dan Suzuki had a specially embroidered, extra wide black belt sent to him from Japan.

The floor of Peter Suzuki's dojo was not of the traditional sort. Instead of the polished wood associated with Japanese dojos, it was covered with a green carpet and while the soles of the feet could cope, it often burnt any softer skin that rubbed against it. It looked much larger than it actually was because two walls were covered from floor to ceiling with mirrors. While seeing your own reflection is sometimes handy while practising a kata, I found it disconcerting – Bruce Lee entering the mirrored maze in *Enter the Dragon* came to mind. Clinton and I got on with our stretching exercises as more and more students came into the cramped dojo. We were wondering just how many more could get in when Peter Suzuki arrived just behind a flustered young man wearing a white belt.

The dojo fell silent as we saw Suzuki's expression: he looked in a foul mood. I was busy looking at his arms as there was a rumour that one was a good deal shorter than the other. The story went that the teenage Suzuki was continually getting involved in brawls in the rougher parts of his hometown in order to test out his techniques. One day his instructor decided to teach him some humility and once the rest of the class had held down the young braggart, the instructor promptly broke his arm. I did wonder if it were true – but one of his arms did look shorter. We were called into lines: brown belts at the front, purple and green in the middle rows and white belts at the back. It was an example of inverted logic as it seemed more sensible to me to have the beginners at the front so they could see more of what the instructor was doing. With our heels together and hands by our side, we stood to attention and waited for the command to kneel but Suzuki had some other business to attend to first. He called the young white belt who had bustled in ahead of him to come to the front of the class and ordered him to stand to attention. Without another word, Suzuki slapped him across his face. The young man stood there perplexed: was this some sort of test? The second slap was even harder and almost spun the young guy around. Again he looked at his sensei with confused eyes: was he supposed to block the strikes? The third slap had so much force behind it that it even made me wince and now the befuddled novice had tears streaming down his reddened cheeks.

"You cry!" exclaimed Suzuki. "You crybaby! I don't teach crybaby. You go . . . Go!"

As the crushed and blubbering man hurried out, Clinton and I exchanged bemused glances as we silently wondered what was going on. It turned out that in the young man's rush to get to the dojo, he had brushed past his sensei on the stairs – but in his haste he was completely unaware he had done so. The absence of an apology was viewed by Peter Suzuki as evidence of a lack of respect that needed correcting but I was of the opinion that Suzuki's method of reminding the novice of his manners was more in the line of a Japanese POW camp guard, rather than a man who made his living by teaching karate to students who paid him rather well.

Finally, Suzuki barked, "*Seiza!*" We went down onto our knees and then heard the word most western students hated to hear when in that position: "*Moksu.*"

Moksu is supposed to be a period of meditation in which the mind is prepared for the exertions that lay ahead. For a Japanese person, kneeling is a normal position but after a few minutes most gaijin students find themselves struggling to retain a calm facade as pain shoots through the lower limbs and at the YMCA we were only kept in that position for a short time. Peter Suzuki, on the other hand, kept us kneeling for fifteen, long, minutes and there was a common exhalation of relief when we heard: "*Yame.*" For the next twenty minutes we went through a farcical attempt of going through some basic techniques. Combinations of kicks were almost impossible because of the lack of space, especially when a back-kick was involved. Those in the middle row risked getting their teeth knocked out by the karateka directly behind them. What was happening in Suzuki's dojo epitomized for me what could go so wrong about clubs that were run for the profit of the instructor; while so many at a grading were good for commercial reasons, it did nothing for anyone's karate.

Eventually, as the exercise became so obviously untenable, Peter Suzuki called a halt and told the brown and purple belts to take a break outside while he examined those who were taking grades up to fourth kyu. For over an hour we waited in the changing room, doing our best not to let our muscles stiffen. Glum-faced green belts were making their way downstairs as we ventured up to the dojo. Peter Suzuki was seated at a small desk scribbling on grading forms until he looked up and dismissively gestured for us to stand to one side. The woman who had taken our money and licences was now in a gi and called out our names. There were twelve of us in all: four purple belts taking their first brown belt grading; four third kyus taking their second brown; and Clinton and I with two others taking first kyu, the final examination before first dan, black belt.

The woman, who wore a black belt, called out the techniques we were to perform up and down the dojo while Suzuki crossed his arms and looked bored by the whole affair. I did my best to block him from my mind but one purple belt got completely flustered and seemed to forget everything he had learned up until that point. His confidence was even more undermined when Suzuki made two theatrical strokes of his pen on the sheet in front of him.

The two other brown belts who were taking the first kyu examination with Clinton and me, were up first to do their pair-work. With snap and precision in every technique they performed, they went through the sanbon gumite (three-step sparring); ohyo gumite (semi-free fighting); and kihon kumite (the moves which encapsulate Ohtsuka's theories about budo and karate in particular). They had set a very high standard. Clinton and I were a lot more perfunctory in comparison and I thought we might have scraped a pass. Next was the kata; again the other two went first and gave a very controlled display in which they utilised kiais and pauses for dramatic effect, and used facial expressions to give the impression that they were really fighting four opponents. No YMCA karateka had ever entered a kata competition, never mind win one and it would be fair to say that our kata did not reach the same standard of the other pair. Along with Hironori Ohtsuka himself, most of my fellow members were of the opinion that kata was a means to an end – and not an end in itself. When Ohtsuka had originally established his own style of karate, the Wado Ryu syllabus contained only nine katas, which is remarkably few when compared to other styles. Later the number grew to fifteen and according to senior Japanese Wado Ryu instructors, he had considered including a long Nahate kata called 'suparinpei' but forgot it halfway through and so did without it. While his detractors would point to the affair as evidence of Ohtsuka's lack of knowledge at that time, to me and many others, it illustrated his priorities as he trained men in preparation for war.

"Right," called the woman, "all we have remaining is jiyu

— Chapter Fourteen —

Rigidness means a dead hand; flexibility is a living hand.

Miyamoto Musashi — The Water Book

PERHAPS WINNING IS not always a good thing, as it can change people – and not for the better. Britain had triumphed over Argentina over the Falklands/Malvinas and brought flags hanging out of many windows in the tower block in which I lived and on lampposts which lined my normal route to work. The gang of skinheads held noisy celebrations somewhere in the flats above me – as though they themselves had won the war. I was keeping an eye on them, without saying anything about it to Hilda, as I had put them on the top of my list of suspects as regards the culprits who had stolen and then burnt my car. In truth, part of me wanted them to be guilty so I could vent my anger on them. I had watched them from a distance strut around the place with a swagger I had not seen before. There were reports of them beating up a couple of lads during their revelry because they looked like 'Argies' – more likely they were a pair of unfortunate Asian men. When I heard that I gave up trying to understand just what was behind their hatred of people they did not even know. It was as I was packing my gi that it occurred to me that they had been caught up in an atmosphere that must have been similar to that which pervaded Japan in the 1930s. Was it that Hironori Ohtsuka and the other martial artists who had joined the Black Dragon Society – and who had been revered by so many generations of their followers – were little different in their outlook from the bigoted gang of skinheads who lived above me? It was a sobering thought and one I chose not to dwell upon.

The events during – and in the immediate aftermath of – the short war had only served to alienate me even further from many of the people who I lived amongst. When the Argentinian battleship 'The Belgrano' was sunk, with the cost of hundreds of lives, a sizeable proportion of my workmates celebrated the news as if they had learned of a football result. A plethora of Union Jack flags hung from the girders in the factory and made me wish that my life was as it had been only months before and that Hilda was not expecting our baby: that way I would have resigned or got myself fired. It may have seemed strange that as a person who studied an art that was borne out of warlike impulses, I was opposed to the war but in my twenty-year-old head the matter was a simple one: people whom I did not like also happened to be the people who were all too readily caught up in the jingoism and xenophobia, while the people for whom I had most regard, if not so open as I was in their opposition, were at least quietly questioning the morality of the war. The people who offended me the most were the likes of Fat Bert, who I had down as a member of the National Front, who came to work with a plastic bowler hat which was painted red, white and blue and the small band of men who had tattoos of bulldogs etched onto their arms with 'Falklands '82' underneath. Thankfully my mate Mick was not getting involved in the fevered nationalism: he had enough sense of achievement derived from his Shotokan not to bask in the reflected glory of a victory many thousands of miles away. That is if there was any glory, or victory, in what I perceived as an unjustified waste of human life.

Mick had warned me against being too vocal in my opinions as he feared something dropping on my head from a great height as I walked through the factory but on passing a queue of men waiting to clock out, I could not resist raising a fist and shouting

"Viva Malvinas!" A torrent of abuse came back at me. Mick shook his head and muttered that he wished I had kept my mouth shut and that I was only drawing trouble on myself. I knew he was right but rather than admit to it, I asked if he were turning up at the dojo as planned. "You lot have kept me waiting long enough, and it's about time someone went down there and showed you some real karate," he joked.

*

Supervised by Eddie Cox, I was putting the beginners' class through a simple combination technique while rhythmically counting out, "Ichi . . ni . . san . . shi . ." when I peered through a window and caught sight of Mick. He was standing by the wrought iron gates at the front of the building and taking in the sights. I tried not to laugh but I could see him looking at the scrap of paper I had given him as he scratched his head and looked at the line of women standing across the road. He was greatly relieved to see men turning up in karate gis and tracksuits and followed them inside.

Mick had made a concerted effort to come and train at the YMCA since he had started a club of his own. I had cleared his visit with my sensei and made sure to put the word around that a *friend of mine* would be training with us. Not that Mick was in any great danger: since the club's second win at the British championships there had been a certain maturing of attitudes. A karateka coming from another club to train with us was now seen as a compliment, rather than someone throwing down a gauntlet that was to be picked up and slapped forcefully across his face. The Saturday fighting class would have been a different matter but I was sure Mick would find one of the evening sessions challenging and rewarding. Although he practised Shotokan, the fighting aspect is common to nearly all the schools of karate (with the notable exception of Shotokai, which continues to adhere to Funakoshi's dictate that forbade sparring) and he hoped to pick up a few useful tips to pass onto the members of his club.

When Mick entered the dojo he fidgeted nervously as he felt

himself being scrutinised by curious eyes. I wandered over to him and told him to relax. "I'm trying," he said. "It's just so strange being amongst so many . . . you know."

"Good fighters?"

"No . . . You know."

The skin on Mick's face had become taut and pale. I hazarded another guess. "Black people?"

"Keep your voice down," he replied, looking over his shoulder. "Is this what it feels like when you're amongst white people?"

"It's had its uncomfortable moments but judging by your face, no, not really."

He responded with a nervous smile as the sensei ordered us into lines. At first I did not know whether to admire Mick's honesty or be irritated with him: he had known of the racial make-up of the club and I wanted to ask him what was the issue all of a sudden. It was neither the time nor the place for this sort of conversation but it did make me wonder about Declan Byrne's experiences when he had first entered the YMCA dojo, as, like Mick, he too had grown up in an area that was 99% white. Prejudice is not a one-way street and when Declan first arrived he had been given a hard time by the black patrons of the YMCA who were not even members of the karate club. There had been two occasions when groups of young guys had entered the dojo as he limbered up on his own and challenged him to a fight. A third confrontation never materialized after the first challenger received a broken nose and the second was knocked spark out. His continued presence at the YMCA dojo served to confront many preconceptions.

On the command 'seiza' we knelt down. Before the two bows, sensei called out 'moksu' and we dutifully closed our eyes as we supposedly cleared our minds but all I thought about was Mick, his initial reaction, and the chances that he would get through the session unscathed.

When the lesson started, I found myself distracted by Mick's presence. From the corner of my eye I could see that although he was standing a good deal lower than the rest of us, he was coping with the repetitions of combination techniques but his real test would come after we had finished moving up and down the dojo and started to practise with a partner. I moved to pair off with Mick but failed to see Trog's nifty sidestep that put him in front of me. Trog was now a brown belt and although he was two grades below me he still had an attitude that (in his head) the positions were reversed and that he was my senior. I guessed that he also wanted to prove that he was Mick's superior. It was not long before he, in his usual bumptious way, tried to intimidate the outsider but Mick was having none of it and stood his ground and fired back. Luckily for me I was partnering Danny Moore and he knew that Mick was a friend of mine and that I was not concentrating fully on what we were doing. Despite two warnings from the sensei, Trog continued to dole out heavy punishment but while Mick's spirit kept him on his feet I was getting very angry. Except for admonishing Trog, Cox sensei spoke mostly encouraging words as he paced around the dojo while scrutinising his students. "*Yame*," he shouted. "Fifty press-ups, fifty sit-ups and then change partners." Everyone dropped to the ground and we pumped out the press-ups before rolling over onto our backs to complete the sit-ups and then, without skipping a beat, we were back onto our feet, facing our new partner. The pair-work lasted the best part of an hour and luckily for Mick the two changes of partners enabled him to train with Clinton and me – and during that time he had at least been able to learn more than the knowledge of his own pain threshold.

The sensei then told us to put on our pads for the sparring session. As I pulled on mine, I glanced up at Trog and saw him eyeing up Mick as he put on his own leg and instep pads. Trog only had eyes for his quarry as he walked across the dojo and did not see my own nifty footwork until I put myself in front of him. He had really wanted to step around me to get to Mick but after seeing someone else had got to Mick before him, Trog smirked at me and pushed back his shoulders. "Looks like it's me and you then," he said.

The sensei called out that he wanted us to spar softly as relaxation was the key to good karate. Relaxation was a difficult state to attain, especially in a real fight when either anger or anxiety tightens the sinews. Relaxation was the secret of all the great karate masters. Eddie Cox had trained with Ohtsuka and remarked that there had been no tension in his body as he threw a punch until a microsecond before his fist made contact with its target. I had watched the Shotokan master Hirokazu Kanazawa give a demonstration of tai chi in the 1970s as he too sought to bring a softer element to his style of karate. Sakagami once told us that the more we progressed in karate, the shorter our techniques would become. Relaxation was the secret of fighting close up to an opponent and the short devastating techniques, such as the famous one-inch punch, of kung fu masters. It was all about not punching hard but punching softly.

But I knew Trog would not be sparring softly with me. We had exchanged too many insults and he still thought that my position in the first team was rightfully his. From the word '*hajime*' Trog was throwing heavy and hurtful attacks that rendered the exercise of light sparring useless.

He began by firing a combination of hard punches, some dangerously close to my face. I sidestepped and he charged past me as I attempted – but failed – to counterattack. His aggression was a measure of his resentment. To him, I must have appeared as arrogant as he seemed to me and in reality our bout was nothing more than a clash of youthful and inflated egos. I had purposely stoked the anger he now needed to vent – and I needed to extinguish it before I got badly hurt.

"*Yame!*" the sensei shouted angrily, to bring our sparring to an immediate halt. He glared at the two of us and said, "It seems you two don't want to participate in the class as I've instructed." He told the rest of the class to sit down before he added, "But you two stay on your feet."

The rest shuffled backwards and knelt down on the perimeter of the floor to create a fighting area. "For those who don't know," the sensei continued, addressing everyone but Trog and me, "light sparring means light . . . a chance to improve your techniques, improve your timing and distancing without the risk of injury." To us he said, "Okay, get whatever this is all about out of your systems and then perhaps you'll obey my instructions. *Jiyu kumite, hajime!*"

Trog began by throwing a high and powerful mawashigeri (roundhouse kick) in an attempt to remove my head. Moving backwards, I evaded his kick and felt the rush of wind from his foot as it passed my face. Cursing myself for not immediately capitalising on his attack, I punched him hard on his chest and he staggered back as I tried to drop a kakatogeri (axe kick) on his head. The axe kick was later to be banned from competition on account of it being uncontrollable once it began its descent. It had been responsible for seriously injuring several competitors – but I didn't care; we were going to establish who was the better fighter once and for all. The axe kick missed his head and slid down his ample chest, removing a few hairs by the roots. As if he hadn't felt a thing, he retaliated with a punch that caught me on the side of my head. I spun to my left and gave myself enough time and space to recover. There were several more hurtful exchanges, mostly to the body, that had both of us sucking in air but it was a strategy we both employed in order to avoid any chance of the sensei calling a premature halt to the bout. I could see in Trog's eyes that his fight plan was similar to mine: inflict as much pain as possible to the body and then wait for an opening to bring matters to a halt with a single, vicious technique. Trog made his move for victory: he threw a punch to my stomach to get my hands moving downwards before he again attempted a kick to my head. But I was 'in the zone' in which there is no conscious thought. I cannot say how I reacted to Trog's punch to my stomach – only that it did not hit me – and this time I did not step backwards or to the side, I stepped *in* – to deliver a punch to his chin before sweeping his supporting leg from under him. Trog hit the ground, legs and arms sprawled out, as I quickly followed up by stamping on his

129

stomach. The fumikomi technique was controlled, hard enough to hurt but not enough to injure.

"*Yame!*" cried Eddie Cox, with more than a hint of approval in his voice.

The look on Mick's face was one of sheer astonishment and for many years to follow he would often refer back to that fight as the most amazing he had ever witnessed. But he never again trained at the YMCA.

After the lesson I got changed into the ubiquitous black 'monkey' suit of a doorman/bouncer before heading out to my car. Clinton pulled a disapproving face. When he had been offered work on nightclub doors he had laughed and said that unless he was prepared to wear half a dozen sweaters underneath his shirt he would come across as far too scrawny. He also added that he may have been Ewart's brother but there was no way that he was going to become his employee too.

"I thought you were only doing weekends," he said, as we strode across the car park.

"I'm doing all the shifts I can so we can get out of that flat."

Clinton crinkled his lips. "So, what time will you get home?"

"About two," I said.

"And you're doing all this for Hilda and the baby?"

"Yeah," I said, "is there a problem with that?"

"Nah," he said airily, "only with the baby due and Hilda being scared stiff at night, I thought you'd be better off at home." He started to walk away. "That's all I'm saying," he said.

— Chapter Fifteen —

Great and small go together.
Miyamoto Musashi — The Wind Book

WHEN I RETURNED from the Sunday morning run and training in the park, I found the flat was empty. Hilda had not left a note but it was not difficult for me to figure out to that she had gone to her mother's. Since the birth of our daughter life in the flat had been getting her down, it was getting the both of us down.

It was a beautiful day and while looking out of my window I thought I would have been gladdened by it. But for some reason I felt desensitized and even the birth of my daughter Nadine did not have the impact I had expected. From somewhere I was not quite sure about, I had picked up the belief that her arrival would be a life-changing moment for me but in reality I felt somewhat distanced from the event. I had been there for the birth, yet no great wave of emotion washed over me and I certainly did not have the bond with the baby that Hilda immediately felt. In those first few days of fatherhood I feared that I was lacking – that somehow I had been left off the list when it came to having parental attachment. As I had looked down at this little stranger in our small twelfth-floor home, I tried to link her with the large bulge in Hilda's abdomen that I had witnessed growing for what seemed an age. For a while I wondered if the absence of a bond with my daughter was due to karate – that perhaps the disengagement with emotions such as anger or fear while training had impaired my ability to feel other, more tender, emotions. To my relief, as the days turned to weeks there was a gradual change within me that I was not really conscious of until one day, as I gently rocked her, I was suddenly aware that I was experiencing a father's love for his child. Although she was so small and light, I knew she was the heaviest load I had ever held in my arms.

I made myself a cup of tea and sat at the small kitchen table and retreated further into my own thoughts. I was searching for justification for what I had planned for the skinheads who lived above me. But consequences for my family loomed large as I thought about what would have happened if I had taken the opportunity of one reckless act of retribution. On my way home from training a few days earlier I had seen three of the skinheads loitering on the pavement. Their presence had become an unremitting one in our home as Hilda rarely let a day go by without mentioning that she felt threatened by them. They had cast a pall of gloom over us when Hilda and I should have been at our happiest and as I drove past them an urge had gone through me to mount the pavement and run them down. The malicious thoughts were a symptom of my growing frustration that I had yet to find another place to live. Feeling the walls were closing in on me, I picked up my car keys and headed for the front door.

I had driven aimlessly at first and somehow ended up in Birmingham. While traversing the outskirts, I made up my mind and headed for a cinema in Handsworth that every Sunday showed an all-day programme of kung fu films.

It was impossible to avoid my cousin Ewart, Pete and the other guys from the YMCA who observed the Sabbath in the dilapidated cinema, as they always occupied the back rows along with a few members of the Temple Karate Centre and the Shukokai club in Birmingham. I greeted a few of them and then took a seat a few rows down. When I was a teenager, kung fu films were enough to distract me from my troubles in the world outside but whatever was happening on the screen, or in the seats around me, I could not divert my mind from all the concerns I had carried in with me.

132

Maybe it was a sign that I had moved on.

I was feeling cramped when I stood up to leave halfway through the second film. I'd had enough of it and Clinton's words about Hilda being on her own began to haunt me. I knew she would be safe, as her brother would give her a lift from their mother's place but I felt anxious all the same. From an aisle seat near the exit Pete put out his hand asked me how come I was leaving so soon. I told him I had work in the morning. He laughed and whispered, "That never stopped you before."

"Things change," I said.

I got to the door of my flat without any memory of the journey from Birmingham as ideas about what my reception might be had preoccupied my mind. The first indicator that something was wrong was when my key was unable to turn the lock. I bent down and looked through the letterbox but this time there was no chair wedged under the door handle. Again I tried the key and only then it dawned on me that Hilda's growing fear about where we lived had caused her to lock me out.

*

The nightclub was almost empty. There would be no great inrush of customers, or any chance of trouble, until the pubs closed. Trouble, came too often at 'Arches', mostly in the shape of drunken young men who travelled in packs of three or four and without female company. During the few months I had worked on the door, I had begun to think of alcohol as the most dangerous drug in the world. Alcohol made cowardly men brave; the resentful uninhibited in venting their rage; and impotent youths unrestrained when expressing their envy. They were usually most resentful about that "someone else" who had got the well-paid job that they could have done "with their eyes shut"; or jealous of the nice "bird-pulling" car that they were only too happy to scratch with the point of a key. When drunk, they exposed their envy of every man who was quite obviously better endowed and who could chat up women without first going to the expense of downing ten pints of beer. Whatever the other cumulative effects of alcohol had on them, it enabled some to either weep openly that some woman or other did not love them, or alternatively it spurred them to put a beer glass into the face of a man who had let his eyes stray in the wrong direction on overhearing the maudlin rambling. I often lurched between loathing and pitying such men.

Ironically, the best behaved patrons were the Hell's Angels. Once we had acknowledged the importance of their 'colours' they reluctantly acquiesced to the frisking for weapons that was club policy on every night. No one got in without being searched, even the three off-duty detectives that Don Hamilton took great delight in telling either they were searched or they were barred. Bikers' night was the one in which we had collected most weapons, long bayonets mainly, that were always explained away with the excuse it was only a tool for repairing their motorcycles. Frisking for weapons was not something I did readily on Bikers' night after one evening when my fingers ran up and down artificial legs on more than six occasions. The men, who were all around my own age, merely smiled as I drew a sharp intake of breath. "Fell off the bike, mate," they often said by way of explanation.

I joined Declan Byrne on the pavement outside. "Have you seen Clinton lately?" he asked.

"Yeah," I replied, "I called to him before I came here."

"Only, I bumped into him by the shops a few days ago," he said. "How do you think he's doing?" Because he was spending more time teaching at the clubs he had set up with Eddie Cox, Declan only got to the YMCA dojo for the Saturday fighting class and I figured he was just checking up on how the students were progressing. "Great, Clint's in really good form at the club," I said, "and he's training very hard for the national championships."

"I don't mean that sort of form." Declan hesitated and then went on, "He wasn't feeling too well a while back, I was just wondering if that problem has cleared up."

"You know Clinton, he can be a little weird at times, but as I said he's just fine." I answered. I wanted to ask Declan about what

134

had brought on his line of questioning but I had pressing questions of my own that I needed resolving.

"How's Hilda and the baby?" he asked, as he stepped out onto the pavement again.

"They're both fine," I said. "When is yours due?"

"Any day now," Declan said guiltily. "This will be my last shift for a while, so if you want to earn some extra money you can take mine on." Declan had got married the previous year to a tall and very attractive Jamaican woman and had made it clear that he would rather spend his evenings with his pregnant wife and was only working as a doorman as a favour to Eddie Cox. He did not like the job, the club, nor the customers and did little to hide his feelings.

"Sure," I said, immediately aware that Hilda would not be happy about me spending more nights away from home, "I'll cover for you. Declan, can I ask you a personal question? Well, I'm looking more for advice than anything else."

"Fire away. You look like a man with a lot on his mind."

When I had mentioned my plan for visiting retribution upon the skinheads to Chester Morrison, one of the senior black belts, his silence spoke volumes. Needing a more enthusiastic response, I then thought about going over my plan with Declan. "It's about these National Front skinheads who stole and burned out my car, I was talking to Chester about how I'm going to put things right."

"And what do you think Chester was trying to tell you?"

I picked up, by his tone, that the two men had talked about my plan for revenge. Immediately less sure of its soundness, I said, "Well, he pointed out a few flaws in the plan. . . . Which I took on board. I mean, I'm not going to ask for advice and then take no notice of it."

Declan shook his head. "I was going to have a word with you about that. According to Chester, that's exactly what he thinks happened. He told me he was pointing out the craziness about what you've got in mind and you were just nodding your head as if he were advising you on a different way of doing something that is very stupid instead of forgetting all about it. It's stuff that can spiral out of hand, Ralph, and for what, a piece of junk that was only good for the scrap yard?" I scratched my scalp but before I could make a response he continued, "Besides a hunch, what makes you think that the skinheads stole that heap of scrap? You say it's these fellas but how do you know that? All this for a car, from what I saw of it, that wasn't worth a tenner. It sounds as though someone did you a favour, at least you didn't have to pay anyone to come and tow it away. Ralph, if someone had damaged your child or your missus, it would be different, I mean, they are the most important things in your life, right?"

His words had come like a stinging slap across my face. I had so badly wanted the skinheads to be responsible for stealing my car that a trivial matter like proof was something that I was prepared to overlook. "An eye for an eye – and we all end up blind" was something once said to me and maybe it was my own blind prejudice that had led me to a point of considering a violent course of action against the skinheads. I took a deep breath, hoping for a few words that would counter his argument. When nothing came, I said to Declan, "Yeah, you're right." My tongue dabbed the corners of my mouth as if the words had left a bad taste and I said, "Thanks for the chat."

Half an hour before closing time, I wandered back outside to escape the stench of smoke and body odour billowing up the stairway from the bar and dance floor. Getting the punters to go home after a night of drinking was often troublesome and I thought it best if I took in some fresh air to make myself fully alert. I stepped out in time to see Declan turning away three drunk young men. "Sorry, lads," he said, "we're closing in a few minutes."

"We only want one drink," one of them said.

"You've had plenty. Come back another night."

A police van pulled up across the road. "Everything all right?" a cop called to us.

"No problem," Declan called back.

The police van moved on, it was not unusual for them to slowly patrol the streets as the clubs began to close. The three drunk men, all in their early twenties, took themselves a few yards down the road and we watched them as they stood talking to each other for a few minutes after a final request for a drink was met with a curt shake of Declan's head. He was about to say something to me when the police van reappeared and stopped directly opposite the club. A sergeant got out; there was a menacing look on his face as he pulled a soft leather glove over his hand and balled it into a fist. Four other cops exited from the rear and walked towards us. I sensed violence and adrenalin immediately shot through my veins. I fixed my eyes on the sergeant who was leading the group. His eyes met mine as his smile twisted in a contemptuous way – just as he started to veer in the direction of the three drunks. The cops surrounded the young men before they bundled them into an alleyway and out of my sight. But still I heard the smack of leather against flesh, I heard the dull thuds of booted feet striking bodies, I heard the screams of pain and terror echo along the high brick walls. Moments later, the bloodied men were dragged to the rear of the police van and pushed inside. The sergeant got in the front and, turning his face in my direction, he ran his tongue over his teeth and the menacing look returned. I stood motion-less, trying to figure out what the young men could have done to deserve such treatment. Their reaction when refused admis-sion to the club had been good-natured enough and to me it seemed their only crime was to be in the wrong place at the wrong time. Declan snarled as the van moved away.

"I suppose they might've made trouble elsewhere and the cops were looking for them," I said.

"You know," said Declan, "they wouldn't have done that to those blokes if it looked as their though daddy was a solicitor or a doctor, or something."

"Does everything have a political connotation with you?"

"Yep," he laughed, "so let's go and clear this gin joint of the great unwashed and send them back to their hovels."

On the way home, my mind was full of the images of that

evening. When the police had beaten the three men, Declan had looked on impassively and had not displayed any notion of intervening, he knew nothing about them and that they shared the same skin colour meant nothing to him. Yet, I asked myself if they had been three young black guys would I have simply stood by, or would I have intervened because of a misplaced allegiance to a colour of a skin. Did the three men's white skins make what I had witnessed anything less of an injustice?

When the young white men at work had told me that they had also been subjected to police harassment I did not disbelieve them, I simply thought that whatever they were exposed to did not come close to the treatment that black people endured at the hands of the police. But after witnessing the brutality meted out to those three young men I began to wonder about how much of what I thought was a 'black' experience, especially when encountering the police, was also something to do with social status, with what the British call 'class'. I thought back to that Sunday morning walk with Mr. Kovac and understood just a little more of what he had said to me.

— Chapter Sixteen —

They speak of this dojo and that dojo; they are
looking for profit.
        Miyamoto Musashi — The Ground Book

THERE WAS A strangely subdued atmosphere about the 1982 Wado Ryu championships that were held at Crystal Palace in London. As Mick Davies had predicted, the death of the Grand Master Hironori Ohtsuka had turned out to be something of a calamity for the school of karate he had left as his legacy. For years, it had been reported that Tatsuo Suzuki, 8th dan Hanshi, would inherit the title of kancho – but while the prince and 'heir presumptive' had been away from court, there had been manoeuvres to usurp his position.

It was only on the few occasions as I had received a trophy from him that I had exchanged a few words with Suzuki, the man known as 'The Professor' in our dojo; 'professor' being an honorific title bestowed onto an elite of karate masters. I always thought of him as a slightly aloof figure but Eddie Cox, who had once brought him along to a wedding reception, did say with a few drinks inside of him he revealed himself to be a warmer man with a dry sense of humour.

Black belts huddled in groups around the arena and discussed the dramatic events and machinations that had taken place both before and after Ohtsuka's death. In between the elimination rounds, they swapped conjecture and rumours about why it was

Ohtsuka's son Jiro, and not his most famous student, who had become the head of the Wado Ryu style of karate. It turned out that almost a full year before the old man's death there had been moves by the claimants to Ohtsuka's title of kancho. It had been kept from most Wado Ryu students in Europe that Hironori Ohtsuka had been in conflict with Eiichi Eriguchi, the man who had coined the name 'Wado Ryu', and nine months before his death he had founded an organisation called Wado Ryu Karatedo Renmei. After only a few months, as his health failed, he installed at its head his son Jiro. There was another story that Tatsuo Suzuki had been offered the head post but had turned it down in favour of Ohtsuka's son but whether that was true or not, few believed it. The theory that seemed to be gaining most credence amid the hubbub in Crystal Palace was that the seeds of destruction for Tatsuo Suzuki's ambitions, had been sown several years before, during Hironori Ohtsuka's visit to Britain in 1975. It was rumoured that Ohtsuka was not greatly impressed by the performances of Tatsuo Suzuki's British students and he had found the style of karate they were practising was at much variance to his own.

Without doubt, karate had altered once it had left Japan and Wado Ryu in Europe had undergone many changes and modifications since Tatsuo Suzuki had left his homeland. It was said that members of Ohtsuka's entourage had thought that Suzuki's style of Wado Ryu had become too rigid, too similar to Shotokan and that much of its jujitsu roots had been discarded. The counter theory to that was Suzuki had developed a much more successful style and criticisms of it were down to little more than jealousy. Wherever the truth lay, the end product was three separate governing bodies of Wado Ryu: one led by Suzuki, another by Eriguchi and one led by Jiro Ohtsuka who would later change his name to Hironori Ohtsuka II. Personally, none of it affected me, or my karate, but I did think that for an art that was supposed to enable its practitioners to become more wholesome people, it all made for an unedifying spectacle.

The Wado Ryu championships were still without the weight

categories that featured in national all-styles events. The major governing body for the Wado Ryu style in Britain was the *United Kingdom Wado Kai (UKKW)*. It was an organization that had produced not only a team which had dominated British karate for four years but had also yielded the only British-based fighters who were to win the heavyweight all-styles world championship during the twentieth century. Jerome Atkinson, Vic Charles and Jeoff Thompson were not only big men who shared an African-Caribbean heritage but, through their athleticism, they had taken the level of competition technique to new heights during the 1980s.

The Japanese instructors were not slow to claim every bit of credit they could for the success of Wado Ryu students in all-styles events but in reality they had played only a minor part. As a group, they were reluctant to compromise on the few remaining vestiges of what they saw as the budo (martial) aspect of competition karate and consequently the scoring criteria at Wado Ryu tournaments differed somewhat to that of other competitions in that the scoring techniques were allowed to be delivered with a lot more power. While this view was endorsed, in some part, by the YMCA's instructors, it also meant that smaller karateka were always going to be at a disadvantage if they came up against a fighter who could match them for speed and skill but also had thirty or forty pounds of more bone and muscle to put behind a kick or a punch.

Vic Charles had left the *UKKW* some years before and international fighters like Jerome Atkinson, Jeoff Thompson, Neiman Prince and my cousin Ewart no longer bothered entering the individual event. Single style titles really had a ring of 'big fish in a small pond' about them. The titles that counted the most were the ones in which a fighter was pitched against the very best from other schools of karate and the top competitors' lack of interest in the Wado Ryu title devalued it somewhat and was akin to Manchester United, Chelsea and Liverpool not bothering to play in the FA Cup. However, it did mean that fighters of my standard benefited and I fought my way through the elimination rounds until I found myself facing Clinton in the final.

Clinton had fought brilliantly all day and replicated the form he had shown when he had humbled a leading competitor from London in a regional final a month before. Clinton had been so superior that his renowned opponent, who led his own style and association, was reduced to falling to the mat and feigning injury in order to secure a very hollow victory. In between my own bouts, I had watched Clinton as he triumphed over every opponent with ease. He had recovered his speed, a sense of balance that never faltered and a range of techniques that I doubted I could ever attain, no matter how hard I trained. The only advantage I had over him was size. I thought the fight for the Wado Ryu title would be a difficult one for me to win, not only because I had always thought of him as far more naturally talented but also because of the problem I had of thinking of him as an opponent that I badly wanted to beat.

It was late into the evening when we stepped onto our lines to face each other. Our names were announced to the crowd and as their polite applause faded I was still unsure of my tactics as I did not feel that I could go all out against my cousin with my usual aggressive style. Clinton and I had spent most of the evening chatting as though we were at a training session at our own dojo. That we were about to fight each other for the most prestigious title either of us had competed for so far, in our short competitive careers, had hardly registered. I heard Tatsuo Suzuki, who oversaw the evening's proceedings, call 'hajime', the initial cheers of the crowd and then there was nothing except for Clinton and me. I had never felt like this while in a fight before. We moved around, testing each other out and watching each other's eyes, oblivious to anyone or anything else. There was a strange harmony about our movements, we knew each other so well and had trained together for so long that we effortlessly anticipated one another's next move. Feeling relaxed, because I was not bothered about which one of us won, I attacked with a combination of punches that I anticipated Clinton would avoid before I tried to catch him with a kick to the stomach. I punched with my front hand and pushing forward I followed it up with a gyakuzuki to his face before I launched my kick. But Clinton had not evaded my attack and my second punch caught him squarely on the jaw. On this occasion I was glad that I was not wearing hand pads as the muscles in my arm tightened the instant my knuckles touched his flesh and I managed to pull back the punch before it was delivered with full force. Clinton's head snapped back. It was as if his feet were cemented to the floor as his spine arched backwards. I heard '*Yame!*' and stopped immediately. I looked to Clinton and saw that strange look in his eyes again. I did not know if he were asking me did I really want the title so badly that I would hurt my best friend, or if he were asking himself what was he doing there. I had seen him do this sort of thing before, though never during a contest, when his mind seemed to wander off to somewhere very far away with a disconcerting suddenness and I kept looking at him for some indication that he was aware of what was going on.

Tatsuo Suzuki's hand shot in my direction and indicated that I had been awarded a point but at that moment I almost said to him to take it back, that I did not want it. Clinton gave me a thin smile and his eyes looked clear again. He attacked me with a rapid kick, which jolted me back into fighting mode, and the rest of the bout was far more frenetic. To most of the onlookers it may have looked as though we were fighting in earnest but the contest became something of a sparring session in which none of the techniques were thrown with any real venom. When the final bell rang I was the champion. Clinton congratulated me with an embrace and, although I knew it was a genuine expression of how he felt, at that moment I did not think there was a title that meant less to me.

*

There was a full attendance for the Saturday morning fighting class. Although the windows of the dojo were wide open, the gentle breeze did nothing to dissipate the cloying heat that was generated by our bodies. My gi was drenched with perspiration and the creases in the canvas chaffed my skin as I performed my sixtieth front-kick.

There would be a brief respite after another forty as we changed our stance to execute another hundred kicks with the other leg. After forty or so, the maegeris would lose their snap, muscles would start to burn, then knot in excruciating pain and by the eightieth kick the foot would become a like leaden weight on the end of a leg that felt light and powerless. Yet, the count carried on remorselessly and despite all the voices in my head that told me to stop, I never did until I heard the instructor call "*Yame.*"

Some weeks had passed since my win at the Wado Ryu championships and Clinton had not resumed training. I had gone around to his house on several occasions to persuade him to come training with me and each time we would laugh and joke but he always had an excuse about why he could not go to the dojo. There had been times in which, as I was talking to him, he would leave me and abruptly retreat to a darkened room to watch TV. More worryingly, he was back to working on that old car of his.

"*Yame*, stop," Eddie Cox called, before he told us to form straight lines and prepare ourselves to practise kata. It was peculiar to include kata practise in a fighting class, in fact it had never happened before, but I had the feeling that Eddie Cox was doing so as an element of surprise and to counterbalance the competition training. The inclusion of kata was also asserting that he was still the chief instructor and that we followed the criteria as laid down by him. The other black belts were his juniors and I thought he was letting us know who was in charge by having them go through the same gruelling exertions.

After a strenuous period of blocking and countering our imaginary opponents, Eddie Cox allowed us a short break. I sat on the floor with my back pressed against the cool concrete wall and dabbed the sweat from my eyes until they were drawn to a figure standing in the doorway. It was Clinton. He had a sports bag slung over his shoulder and he waved to me before disappearing into the changing room. I was glad to see him but then I became anxious as I wondered which Clinton had turned up at the dojo. I was worried that he may have arrived to take part in the training:

a fit and well Clinton would have known that anyone appearing more than ten minutes late for a session would not be permitted to train.

My heart sank as he reappeared in his gi, bowing as entered the hall. Seeing Eddie Cox, he momentarily stopped in his tracks and waited for a signal from him. The sensei had not seen Clinton before he had entered the changing room and he appeared to be momentarily unsure of what to do. Clinton took his sensei's hesitation as a sign that he should enter and without needing further prompting, he skirted the hall to close to where I sat before taking up a kneeling position and bowing twice. He then got to his feet and waited for permission to join the class.

Every eye in the dojo turned to Eddie Cox, whose expression had turned from mild bewilderment to one of embarrassment. He walked over to Clinton and rested a hand on his shoulder and talked to him in a quiet voice. Clinton smiled and shook his hand in greeting. As more hushed words were exchanged, Clinton's smile vanished before he wandered back to the door. I tried to attract his attention but he did not see me.

On watching Clinton slink out of the dojo I felt a heaviness in my throat. For an instant, instinct nearly overcame discipline and I almost got to my feet to march over to the sensei and ask him what was going on. But reason overcame my raw emotion and glancing around the room, I became aware that everyone else had been closely watching Clinton's dismissal. Some dropped their heads resignedly and a few stared at me to observe my reaction until Eddie Cox shouted for us to line up once again.

As we performed another kata, I felt Clinton's eyes following me from the corner of the dojo where he stood perfectly still after changing back into his clothes. I willed the lesson to come to an end. I needed to speak to him, if only to offer a few words of comfort.

"*Yame*," cried the sensei. "Straighten your lines." He then ordered us to kneel. As we closed our eyes in meditation, to reflect on the training and what we had achieved, all I could think about was Clinton and his obvious hurt.

"*Moksu yame*," said the sensei and we opened our eyes before bowing twice to bring the lesson to a close. Back on my feet, I spun around looking for Clinton. The sun was blazing through the windows and I was momentarily dazzled. It took a few seconds for my eyes to refocus and see that Clinton had slipped away.

In the changing room no one thought it appropriate to talk about Clinton. Instead the conversation was centred around a former member and another of my cousins who had been arrested for attempted armed robbery. It was only as the changing room filled with scornful laughter on hearing a description of his capture that I paid any attention to what was being said. The plan had been to hit a wages' delivery at a factory on payday. My jaw tightened as someone chuckled and said that my cousin had decided to go ahead with the robbery even though a member of the gang had not turned up with the getaway vehicle and he had used his girlfriend's car instead.

I was back to being lost in grim thoughts about Clinton for a few minutes until I realized that the changing room had gradually emptied to leave only Eddie Cox and me. I asked him what had happened with Clinton. "I couldn't let him train," he said regretfully. "Not in his state."

"Come on, Eddie," I said, my voice rising, "he needs to get back into the flow of things. You know, do the things he was doing before."

"I know he's your cousin, Ralph, and you're only looking out for him. But it's medical help Clinton needs and not karate. And I can't take the risk of him, or of someone else, getting hurt."

As Eddie was talking to me, in my mind I saw the smile vanish from Clinton's face as he was told that he could not train and right then I felt his hurt. "He was already changed," I retorted. "I mean, we were only doing kata. It wasn't like there was any risk of him getting hurt or somebody hurting him, now was there?"

"Like the time you nearly hurt him?" Eddie said testily. "Like the *UKKW* final when you nearly took off his head with that punch. There have been signs, Ralph, and like everybody else I've been

146

hoping that things had turned around for the guy. But now there's too much risk. Do you think you could've caught Clinton with a punch like that if he was healthy?"

I tightened my lips and nodded. "Yeah, you're right, it's just . . ."

"It's all right," he said sympathetically, "no need to explain. We're all just hoping that he pulls through." He slapped my shoulder and as we began to walk to our cars Eddie tried to lighten my mood by making a joke about my relative who had been arrested because of his own idiocy. I could only shrug my shoulders and Eddie got into his car. I did not care about the man who had brought problems on himself because of his criminal activities, it was Clinton's predicament that was on my mind as I watched Eddie drive away. I began to wonder if Clinton's present state was a cruel twist of nature, or if the environment in which he lived had applied so much pressure that it had finally started to break his mind and spirit. And if Clinton's illness was due to where and how he lived, could it be that I might succumb to the same pressures at some point in the future?

— Chapter Seventeen —

When the clouds of perplexity clear away, there is true nothingness.

Miyamoto Musashi — The Book of the Void

WAS IT ME, or was it the world that was changing so fast? I had gone from a youth preoccupied with karate to a family man, with all the accompanying responsibilities, in only a matter of months. The transition to adulthood in a short space of time would have been difficult enough for me to cope with but it seemed that the world around me had suddenly grown into a much less pleasant place.

Hundreds of workers had been made redundant at other factories in the area and the lack of certainty about what lay ahead for us sent ripples of discontent throughout my workplace. And for the first time, I began to have concerns about whether or not I would have a job to go to in the near future. If I had only myself to look after, or if I were still living with my parents, the spectre of unemployment would have held no fears for me. But I no longer had the option of a solitary life, nor one of dependancy.

I had arrived at the factory's gates in time to find a handful of workers musing aloud amongst themselves on how they would form a picket line. As I walked through the gate, one of them was attempting to start a fire in an open oil drum and his colleagues were too distracted to even notice me. On reaching the maintenance department, my first inkling that things were not about to turn out as I had been led to believe was the absence of

148

Harold the tea-maker. For the first time, in all my years at the factory, I made the tea and had drunk three cups before it dawned on me that no other member of the crew was willing to cross the unofficial picket line.

The day before there had not been a dissenting voice when the maintenance department had agreed not to take action to support for Dave the labourer. The management, who had been spoiling for a fight, thought they had picked on a soft target when they suspended the factory's resident gigolo after he had reported late for work three days in a row. However, the powers-that-be had not counted on Dave's abiding allure with the female employees in the assembly area, who immediately withdrew their labour. Meetings were hurriedly convened all over the factory. The workers in the tool room and the stamp shop agreed with the view of my department in that they would not take part in any action that did not have official union sanction. Privately, more than one had said that they would not be stopping work for a "toe-rag" like Dave the labourer.

I was relieved to see Mick Davies; he had been away on holidays and was unaware of the industrial strife. I filled him in on events over a cup of tea and I thought that he was having second thoughts about crossing the picket line. To prevent him up and leaving, I then mentioned another victory for the YMCA at a tournament during the previous weekend but his response was less than enthusiastic. He replied, "Well, you've done it all before, haven't you?" The conversation became increasingly strained and I was glad for the sound of the buzzer that signalled the beginning of the shift.

There had been a subtle change in my relationship with Mick since I had turned twenty-one. My birthday had held no special significance for me except that my apprenticeship had come to an end. As an apprentice, I had been viewed by those who inhabited the delicate ecosystem of the maintenance department as at the very bottom of the food-chain. Now I had evolved into a fully-fledged tradesman adjustments were required if we were to preserve the delicate balance in the relationships that enabled us to work as a team. But a further threat of destabilisation within our department came in the form of Mr Pearson, a kindhearted man who was the personnel manager. Mr Pearson had always been on hand during my apprenticeship to offer encouragement and I had often wished that he could have been one of my teachers at school. Shortly after I became qualified, he had asked me to consider carrying on with my studies and said that he would arrange for me to have the necessary time off to take the Higher National Certificate course in production engineering. He added that when I passed I could then be inducted into the heady heights of lower management. Naively, I had mentioned Mr Pearson's offer to the rest of the maintenance crew while we were seated at the long table and my 'good' news had been met with stony silence. My decision to take up the opportunity of becoming better qualified had made our relationship difficult for Mick; there was a clear demarcation at the factory between the workers and management and the mere fact that I had expressed an interest in getting promoted had made me a potential member of the 'enemy'.

I was in the stamp shop trying to figure out what was wrong with a machine when the head engineer approached me. "Ralph, there's no need to worry," he said, "but your mother has just rang." In that split second my mind *was* filled with worry as my mother had never before telephoned the factory. I anticipated terrible news about a family member having an accident – or that something even worse had happened. He continued, "She said there was no need to panic but she asked if you would call into her on your way home."

"Did she say what's it about?" I asked.

"Er, no. She just said there was nothing to panic about."

"She's never rang me at work before."

"Look," he said, scanning the near-empty stamp shop, "with all this stuff going on at the gate perhaps it would be better if you clocked out early."

"I don't understand it," I replied. "Everyone agreed to come in and work unless there was proper union backing for a strike."

He smiled at my naivete. "You still have a bit to learn about human nature and factory politics, Ralph. Once you've got this job finished go and see your mom."

It was as I strode through the crowd at the gateway that my eyes met those of Dave the labourer. They shone with resentment. The boos and jeering increased in volume. "Scab! Scab! Scab!" spat some of the men, who relished the chance to pay me back for my "Malvinas" chant. I could imagine how they must have talked as they saw me walk from the factory. "Just shows you, don't it? The Argie-lover has no loyalty to anyone or anything around here."

"Nigger!" snarled Dave the labourer, the supposed cause of all this trouble.

His words cut through the cacophony like a sharp knife. His lips were still quivering as I stopped and stared at him. He rolled his shoulders and ran his fingers through his oily hair as he looked left and right to the men beside him. I stepped towards Dave and the men around him fell silent and moved away. In that instant he knew that he was on his own and that he had to make a quick decision: was it going to be fight or flight? He could tell by the look on my face what my intentions were and as I closed in on him he abruptly turned and ran as fast as his stubby legs could carry him.

*

On my way to my parents' home I had persuaded myself that perhaps it was good news that my mother had for me and maybe my dad had won the pools or a premium bond number had come up. But it was obvious to me that there had been no big money win as I opened the door; the atmosphere was too subdued for there to be good tidings. My mom, who had always worked so hard as a hospital orderly in a psychiatric ward, was asleep in an armchair in front of the television. She had not heard me come in and I spent a moment or two studying her. Her head lolled to one side and my heart skipped a beat until I heard her gently snoring. The sight of her made me so thankful for all her daily sacrifices – but it did also make me wonder if I were capable of doing anything similar for my own child. She would wake in a few minutes and I thought it best to put on the kettle rather than disturb her. Mom stirred as the water boiled. "Hi, Mom," I called out.

"When did you come in?" she asked.

"Just a few minutes ago, while you were nodding off."

"Make a pot of tea, please, son. I'm parched."

"Way ahead of you," I said, as I brought the pot and cups into her.

She put a cup to her mouth with her two hands and rolled her lips after a first sip. "Ah, a nice cup of tea," she sighed, "just what I needed."

I was too anxious to know about why she had telephoned me at work to take a drink. "Mom," I said, "why did you ring the factory?"

Her eyes immediately became sombre and her lips compressed momentarily. "Clinton," she said sadly, "he was . . ."

"Yeah, he was?" I interrupted.

". . . he was brought into hospital again yesterday."

"Back to the Accident and Emergency?"

"No," she said gravely, "he's in the psychiatric ward. He was examined and diagnosed as having schizophrenia."

"I knew it!" I blurted out, sad and yet relieved that a doctor had finally confirmed my suspicions about Clinton's mental health and that he was now in a place where he could receive treatment. I had visited him during the previous week to find him back underneath his old car. Although it was cold and dark, I felt that I had to get down and join him and see just what he was doing. With the aid of a lamp, Clinton explained the difficulty he was having in fitting the gearbox. It only took me seconds to see that the gearbox was for another type of vehicle and I told him so. He dragged himself from under the car and marched into his house. Sensing he would be out again, I waited next to the car and it was not long before he reappeared carrying a bag. I could tell that he was planning to do something that could have had dire consequences. He went past me without a glance and I sped after him, demanding for him to tell me where he was going and what was in the bag. When there was no response we ended up wrestling with one another on the pavement. He had been heading for Leslie's house with a machete in the bag. After calming Clinton and guiding him back to his house, I went to find out why Leslie had sold Clinton a gearbox that could not possibly fit his car. Leslie explained that he and Errol had told Clinton that there was no way he could use that gearbox but he had insisted that they sell it to him. Leslie was dismissive when I told him about the machete but I knew I had saved someone from getting seriously hurt – or worse – that night.

My mother's news that Clinton had been diagnosed with schizophrenia prompted me to ask about the nature of the illness. "Schizophrenia," I said, "isn't that split-personality and someone going totally insane?"

"Don't be silly," Mom replied. "You'd be surprised at the amount of people walking the streets with mild cases of schizophrenia. Clinton will be all right once he's receiving the proper treatment, it's when this illness goes untreated that things can turn very bad."

"Bad for who?"

Mom raised a reproachful eyebrow. "The person with the illness, of course."

I drank my tea to give myself time to think of a question that was not as stupid as my first two. "How is he now?" I asked.

"A bit drowsy and confused because of the drugs he's on. But he was asking for you."

"I'll try and see him in the next few days," I said. I brought the cup back to my lips to try and hide my embarrassment as I realized that I was already making excuses about not finding the time to visit him. The hospital was in walking distance from where I lived. "Anyway," I added, to break the uncomfortable silence that had settled between us, "at least he'll get the treatment he needs. When did you find out about him?"

"His mother rang me last night and I went into see him today. It was so sad to see so many young men in there." Her voice began to waver and she shook her head as a tear threatened. "I had a talk with his mom and she reckons that Clinton's troubles started with karate and she says that someone told her that he was once knocked out. Do you know anything about that?"

While it did not happen at every session, someone getting rendered unconscious was not that unusual at the karate club. A few professional boxers had trained with us from time to time and muttered their doubts about our sanity after viewing the amount of punishment that we sometimes dished out to one another. I, along with several others, had been kayoed but had not suffered any lasting repercussions. "No, I don't recall Clinton ever getting knocked out," I replied – and almost immediately I thought about the punch I had landed on him with during the Wado Ryu national championships. "We control the punches, you know, Mom, so people don't get hurt."

"Ralph!" she snapped back, "don't take me for a fool. I haven't forgotten all those times you came home with a swollen face, or that time I found blood in the toilet. Do you really think that all those kicks and punches haven't affected you?"

"Mom, it's not karate that had made Clinton ill!"

Mom snorted sceptically. "Me and your father have been talking. We think you should consider giving up karate and think of Hilda and little Nadine a bit more."

I bit my lip in frustration: I had intended to ask my father for a loan towards a deposit on a house but there was no way I could approach him now, as I could easily guess the one condition he would attach to lending me the money. "Look, Mom, karate didn't turn Clinton this way," I insisted. "He's always been a bit eccentric, even as a kid he'd do some strange things. I'm telling you, Mom, karate didn't make Clinton the way he is."

Mom fixed me with a stare and said, "And I remember you telling your sister that karate is a test of the mind as well as the body. It's easy to see the damage when the body fails the test but what happens to the mind, can you tell me that?"

— Chapter Eighteen —

*If your opponent thinks of mountains, attack like the
sea; if he thinks of the sea, attack like mountains.*
Miyamoto Musashi — The Fire Book

BY THE SPRING of 1983 I was getting used to the radical changes
in my training regime. I had finally faced up to the likelihood that
Clinton would not be putting on a karate gi for a considerable
time. But if anything, my sessions at the dojo had increased in
intensity as I fully immersed myself in the training. I once heard
an older karateka say that it was not only his physical decline that
had affected his performance in the dojo but also his waning
powers of concentration as he became less able to block from his
mind the problems he had in the world outside. However, once
I entered the dojo I became a karateka and nothing else and for
a brief time I was no longer a father; an employee; I was no longer
somebody's friend. But when the sessions ended I was confronted
by the hard facts that I was still living in that high-rise flat with
my family; I was working at a place that I found increasingly hard
to bear; and I was letting down my closest friend.

Since his discharge from the hospital, I had not visited nor telephoned Clinton's home. It was not that I did not care, perhaps
it was because I cared too much. I had managed to visit him once
while he was in the psychiatric ward, when Hilda had accompanied me and brought him a trifle to eat. Clinton had been so
overcome by this little act of kindness that he wept openly. I

155

thought then that I had never witnessed a sadder sight.

His mother's theory that Clinton's schizophrenia had been brought about by a knockout blow while training was one that did not stand up to serious scrutiny, yet it lingered in my mind for a time. The punch I had landed on his jaw during the Wado Ryu championships was one I replayed over and over until I angrily reminded myself that not only was the punch controlled and had not rendered him unconscious – but also that Clinton had shown signs of having a mental illness a considerable time before that bout. What remained with me longer were the questions I asked myself about my unwillingness to visit him. I hated to admit it but I stayed away from my cousin because of a raw and base emotion called fear.

Karate training may have helped me to overcome fear of physical pain or confrontation but it did nothing for the emotional anxiety I felt when I thought of Clinton's plight. We had known each other for nearly twenty years, almost all of our lives. We were tied by blood, we had grown as friends and in our camaraderie we could anticipate each other's words and thoughts; in a way, we *shared* rather than anticipated. It was not as though I merely knew his moods by the way he moved or by a small facial expression, I *felt* them. During the times when I saw him abruptly withdraw from the world there had been a reaction inside of me but I had pretended to myself that I was confused about what I felt. But in truth, every time I had witnessed such an episode I had felt scared that a constant and predictable presence in my life had been some-times turned into a stranger who merely resembled him. The longer I stayed away from Clinton the greater grew my sense that I had let him down. I knew that I would have to go and see him, it was just that I did not know when.

*

As reigning British champions, the YMCA karate club had been invited by the local council to put on a demonstration at a fair that was held annually in the town's largest park. Neither Eddie Cox nor any of the black belts were keen as the English national all-styles championships were approaching and the training at the dojo had reached new levels of intensity. It was decided, therefore, to have the junior under-15 class put on a short exhibition of what a Wado Ryu class entailed as Eddie Cox supervised them.

The day did not start off as planned. Most of the YMCA's senior members had turned up to show support and had wandered into the marquee that housed an old style boxing booth. But rather than inviting the onlookers to do a few rounds with a boxer, the members of the audience were challenged to put on the gloves and fight with one another. Unaware that members of the YMCA karate club had just entered the tent, and egged on by other members of his gang, a large white man had ducked in between the ropes and launched a tirade of racial abuse at a young black boy, who was barely half his size, and dared him to come and fight. The insults became too much for Eddie Cox who jumped into the ring and only reluctantly put on the gloves. The fight did not last long: the Marquis of Queensberry rules meant nothing to Eddie who struck the man behind his ear with the edge of his hand and followed up the blow with a knee to the solar plexus. Pandemonium threatened to break out as the rest of the man's gang prepared to rush the ring – until they realized that Eddie Cox was far from being alone.

An hour later, I was wandering over to where the demonstration was being held when I met up with Chester Morrison who told me that he had just seen Clinton. "He was asking for you," he said.

My feet felt increasingly hot and heavy as I searched the fairground. I became oblivious to the heaving throng, the blaring music and the smell of diesel: I had set my mind on finding Clinton and nothing was going to distract me. An ache appeared in my chest after I had paced around the fair three times and had caught no sight of him. Now I felt the weight of the people pressing in on me, now I heard the deafening cacophony, now I smelled the foul odours. Deflated, I thought about heading for the tennis courts to watch the demonstration, unsure if I really should have been disappointed about not finding Clinton, when a pair of strong arms reached around from behind and grabbed me in a bear hug. I had been too lost in my thoughts to instantly work out what was happening and I was further confused by the pair of wet lips and the accompanying sensation of prickly stubble against my cheek. My feet left the ground and for a moment the air was being squeezed out of me. "Put me down!" I gasped.

When my feet touched the ground again and the arms around me fell away, Clinton said, "Sorry, Ralph, I didn't mean to wind you."

I was so shocked by his appearance that all the excuses I had rehearsed about why I had not visited him vanished in an instant. His hair was neatly combed and his clothes were clean and pressed but his face was very bloated, and those eyes that were once so fiery and vibrant were now dull and exuded little more than a lethargic delight that we were together once more. He stepped forward and hugged me again. There were no questions from him about where I had been in his time of need and my guilt began to feel like a physical weight inside of me.

Awkwardly, I returned his embrace. "How are you keeping?"

"Where's Hilda and the baby?" he replied, ignoring my question.

"Over by the pond. They'll be watching the demonstration in a minute, are you coming?"

"Yeah, man, let's go," he said. "I've really missed you guys."

As we walked to the tennis courts, he linked arms with me. I immediately felt embarrassed by his actions and then by my own reaction as I instinctively pulled away from him. Partly it was a macho thing: I had been conditioned to think that men did not go around openly showing affection for one another but also it was something Clinton had never done before and his loss of inhibition was unsettling.

A round of applause followed the chorus of kiais and served to let us know that the demonstration had already started. I looked around but could not see any sign of Hilda and Nadine before I sat down next to Clinton at the end of a row of red plastic chairs. As the youngsters performed a series of fighting techniques, he said loudly, "Do you remember when they were us? The handsome one over there is me. The one with the long head, that's you. The little cheeky one that looks like a rat, that's Leslie."

Eddie Cox looked over to where all the noise was coming from and made a small grimace before he called a halt to the pair-work and ordered the young students to perform a kata. As he counted, the youngsters performed a single technique and Clinton threw back his head and roared with laughter, so loudly that several of the youngsters missed the sensei's count and lost their place within the sequence of moves. Now I was embarrassed for Clinton and worried that he was about to make a spectacle of himself. "Hey, Clint," I murmured into his ear, "how about if we head back to the fair?"

"Oh, okay. But what about Hilda and the baby?"

"We'll see them later on," I said, gently taking him by the arm and guiding him back to the fairground. The short walk became agonisingly slow and something tore at my heart as I watched him plodding while remembering how confident his stride had been when we were teenagers. The changes I saw in him then was everything I had feared most. Clinton stopped and said, "Ah, that's what I want to go on."

It took a moment for me to realize what he was talking about. "The Gravity Wheel? Oh no, Clint, you can't go on that."

"Why not?"

I wanted to say that I had seen plenty of people stagger from it feeling very nauseous – and that they were not on potent medication like he was. "Well," I mumbled, "it looks scary to me. Let's go find the dodgems, eh?"

"Nah! You think I'm scared of that? I'll show you," he said forcefully.

"Don't be crazy," I groaned, and immediately regretted my choice of words. Short of taking hold and grappling with him, I did not know how to stop him and the last thing I wanted was a physical confrontation with Clinton. He tottered off and all I could do was wave as he beamed a smile at me from within the circular metal cage. The diesel engine at its centre belched out a cloud of black smoke toward the clear blue sky and the cage began to turn. His smile was still there during the first couple of revolutions but as the cage picked up in speed his face became indistinct to me. The screams started as the metal supports fell from under the pairs of feet and it was only the centrifugal force that kept the Gravity Wheel's occupants from falling. Around and around it went and all I could do was join in with those spinning around in wishing it would quickly come to a halt. It was to my great relief when the diesel engine coughed a final column of black smoke, the wheel began to decelerate and the occupants stopped screaming.

I watched fretfully as they clambered out. Clinton walked toward me on unsteady legs and I moved to meet him on seeing that he did not look too good. He was impassive at first and then his shoulders jerked before he folded as the first of the vomit left his mouth. Some of it hit my leg but more of it hit an unfortunate girl on her back. Those who were close by stumbled and pushed others in their anxiety to evade the projectile vomit. Enraged, the girl turned and screamed, "You dirty bastard!" By this time Clinton was on all fours, retching and coughing. For a few seconds the people who encircled him silently observed the pitiful sight at their feet as he continued convulsing. Then, as he stopped heaving, a few of them laughed before they moved on while muttering amongst themselves. My hands were shaking as I took Clinton by the shoulders and lifted him gently to his feet. "Oh, Clinton, Clinton," I sighed, "you're covered in sick, man. Come on, I'll take you home so you can get out of those clothes."

"I'm not going anywhere until I see Hilda and the baby."

"We'll come back once you've changed. You don't want them to see you like this, do you?"

He dropped his chin and looked to the vomit still dripping from his front. "No," he said quietly, "no I don't."

We drove to his house in silence, the putrid smell in the heat almost overpowered me and I had felt like throwing up on several occasions. His mother bravely tried to make light of what had happened as Clinton went to his room but I could tell that she was deeply upset. I told her that I had to get home to change out of my clothes and that I would then come back for Clinton. She smiled appreciatively but I think we both knew that I did not have it in me to return that day.

*

During the following months I continued to call on Clinton before I reported to 'Arches'. I nearly always found in him in the same darkened room gazing blankly at a television. More often than not he would tell me that door work was dangerous and that I ought to find another means of earning extra money. Just as he had been when we were kids, Clinton always seemed to put my well-being before his own.

It was nearing closing time at the nightclub when I began to go through my little ritual of re-energizing myself before I had to go downstairs with the others and persuade the patrons to leave. I was not in a good mood. I exhaled heavily as I stood outside the nightclub's entrance and wondered when the gloom would lift.

The evening had not got off to a good start. After chasing around the flat for a clean shirt, while Hilda looked on in her usual silent disapproving way, my visit to Clinton had left me morose and brooding. His younger brother Vernon had told me that he was out with "some girl". I knew the woman Vernon was talking about and thought that she could be very bad news for Clinton. She was not an unattractive woman but her features were a little too sharp and her eyes were a little too cold for my taste. In the one and only time I had met her, I figured that she was just the sort of woman Clinton did not need in his present state and I had tried to tell him so in a very subtle way. Obviously, I had been either too subtle or simply ignored. I drove to the nightclub arguing with myself that I was being overprotective about my cousin and that he did not need me interfering. Clinton had more than enough brothers to act as his keeper.

My mood grew even gloomier when Declan Byrne told me that he was giving up working at the nightclub. His reason for leaving made me feel that I should reappraise some of my own attitudes.

"Why now?" I asked him.

"Ah, well, I told Cox that I was only doing this until the business with the Italian crowd was sorted. I'm teaching most evenings and I'd prefer to be home with my wife and baby rather than staying out all night and dealing with a place I wouldn't piss on if it was burning. I'm not cut out for this, I'm just too soft for this game."

Since he had got married there had been a marked change in Declan; for a start he no longer pounded his fists against a makiwara when there "was nothing on TV". But I smiled at his use of the word 'soft', only men with nothing to prove would describe themselves in that way. 'Arches' was a venue where there was lots of trouble and it did mean that our demeanour while on the door had gradually become more aggressive. This did not sit well with Declan's personality, nor personal morality. He was an affable man – but affability can be construed as a weakness by men who are out looking for trouble, which then led to the troublemakers being forcibly corrected in their wrong-headed notion. While Ewart may have made an exception for a pretty girl, by the look on his face everyone entering a club where he was working knew exactly what was going to happen if trouble broke out. And perhaps Declan's use of the word 'soft' was not misplaced. In both Chinese and Japanese martial arts there is the theory that the hard (*go*) cannot exist without the soft (*ju*), and that a karateka has to attain and understand both elements if he is to be an effective fighter. In Wado Ryu we were taught that the muscles had to be soft, or relaxed, and only tense at the moment of impact if a blow was going to hit hard – and sometimes Declan had hit people very hard indeed. Violence did not particularly trouble him, but the context in which it took place did. I knew he was bothered about an incident which had occurred a few weeks before and that it continued to prey on his mind. He had just forcibly ejected a man who had attended the Bikers' night when a tall man came off the street with two others behind him and tried to force his way in. Declan had struck him in such a way that if he had not pulled the blow at the last split-second there could have been dire repercussions. As it was, the man spent a night in a hospital. The following night the man's two colleagues turned up to complain to the management about the disproportionate use of force. To my surprise, Declan apologized profusely and subsequently allowed the man free admission and bought him a drink in an attempt to make amends. He later admitted to me that putting out the biker only seconds before had clouded his judgement and he had overreacted. He sighed, "It was all happening in slow-motion and as my hand shot out, I thought: hit this bloke and you're doing serious time in prison, Declan, and you won't be seeing your beautiful baby for a very long while. And for what? To stop these piss-heads getting even more pissed? See, I don't give a damn if these fellas knock the hell out of one another, or whatever else they want to do. So why should I turn up here to be offended instead of staying at home with my wife and our gorgeous little daughter and putting my feet up?"

What Declan had said to me did not initially change my attitude to working the doors – I was convinced it was a grim necessity for me – but I was dwelling on my priorities again when he nudged my arm and said that it was time to start moving the customers out.

Once the club was cleared, Don Hamilton came over to me and broke the news that there had been a very serious fight at another nightclub across town involving an old acquaintance of ours. Tony was a brutal young man of around my age and I could not find it within me to have any sympathy for him when Don told me that he had lost a leg after it had been struck with a machete. I had first met Tony when were youngsters following my older cousins' arrangement to have a bare knuckle fight with him after school. They had embarked on an entrepreneurial venture by matching me with boys of my age, or a little older, and placing bets on the outcome. I had made the mistake of winning my first couple of fights, and thereby making money for them, and I was too afraid to refuse when they told me to report to the park. Tony was the strongest boy I had ever fought. He was stocky and at fourteen he had the corded forearms and biceps of a grown man. We had battered one another to a standstill and much to my cousins' displeasure the fight was declared a draw. It was no surprise to me when, as the years went by, I heard of Tony's growing reputation for violence. He was a man bereft of affection or respect for anyone, or anything, except for his collection of cars.

"So, what was the fight over?" I asked Don.

"What do you think?" Don snorted, "a woman, of course."

I drove back to the flat that night thinking about what Declan had said about wanting to spend more time with his family and Don's report of another senseless act of violence in the town. I thought about Tony lying in a hospital at the age of twenty-two with only one leg. At one point in our lives we had been very similar in our attitudes to violence and perhaps it was the discipline of karate that had saved me from a similar fate. Not for the first time I contented myself with the thought that I was going home in one piece to my family – and that was all that mattered.

— Chapter Nineteen —

*The spirit of the warrior becomes like water. Water
adopts the same shape as its container; sometimes it
is a trickle, sometimes a raging sea.*
Miyamoto Musashi — The Ground Book

THE WAVES OF disruption that had come about in Wado Ryu
karate as a result of the death of Hironori Ohtsuka had taken a
little more than a year to ripple from Japan and lap at the door
of the YMCA dojo. Rumours had been circulating that there was
an impending split amongst the Japanese instructors of the *UKKW*
and that some were preparing to withdraw their support for Tatsuo
Suzuki in favour of Jiro Ohtsuka, who was now being feted as
the foremost authority and rightful successor to his father.

Declan Byrne had not been slow on passing judgement on the
whole, rather tawdry affair and was sceptical that Jiro Ohtsuka
had been elevated above Tatsuo Suzuki purely on his abilities as
a karateka. Declan recounted the time that Jiro had made many
headlines in the British press after a demonstration of sword
defence with his father at the 1975 *UKKW* championships. The
razor-sharp blade of the samurai sword had almost severed the
thumb of the eighty-three-year-old master but while he had
stoically carried on with the demonstration and had shown no
distress in its aftermath, Jiro had fainted at the sight of the wound
and had ended up being taken to a hospital in the same ambulance as his father. No one who had ever trained with Tatsuo Suzuki

could ever imagine him fainting at the sight of blood.

A number of the senior grades at the YMCA preferred not to get involved with the machinations that seemed to be engulfing the British section of Wado Ryu and it was decided that the YMCA should leave the *UKKW* and set up a small but independent association of karate clubs. It may have made sense at the time but it was a move that was to be replicated many times in other styles during the 1980s and would do much to undermine Britain's long-term success in international karate contests.

The first sign of the downside of such a move was at the English all-styles championships. We were drawn against the *UKKW* team and defeated them quite convincingly but we lost in the final: the Wado Ryu association team that had dominated British karate no longer existed and its place were two teams that were not quite as good in their constituent parts as they had been as a whole.

I had come second to Jerome in the heavyweight category at the English championships and as it was my first senior national competition I was quite pleased, for once, to return home with a silver medal. There was talk about an invite for me to train with the senior British squad, which had won the world championships in Taiwan the previous year, if I did nearly as well at the British all-styles championships. I wanted to test myself against the best in the world but I was still unsure if I had the ambition to compete for Britain and I contented myself with the thought that the three best heavyweights in international karate were based in England and to win a domestic title while they were competing would be a world-class achievement.

At the following British championships, everyone turned up at Crystal Palace eagerly anticipating the heavyweight final as it surely had to involve two out of those top three competitors but the world champion Jeoff Thompson had injured his back and was unable to compete. With Jerome Atkinson and Vic Charles at opposite ends of the draw, it looked as though they would meet in the final. I was in Jerome's section and was scheduled to meet him in the quarterfinal until disaster struck when Jerome's bad knee gave way during one of the preliminary rounds. It had intermittently plagued him for six years and would be a significant factor in his decision to retire from competition karate after winning the world championship in the following year. However, there was a silver lining in Jerome's injury for me in that, now he was out of the competition, I had a far easier path to the semifinals.

As predicted, Vic Charles was waiting for the winner of my semifinal bout. I was facing an international fighter whom I had previously beaten and I was looking forward to pitting myself against someone of the calibre of Vic Charles. Even though he would not win his world title until after Jerome had retired, Jerome had often said that out of all those he had fought alongside, Vic was the greatest karate competitor he had ever seen. This is slightly different to being the greatest fighter but within the rules as laid down by the world governing body – and despite other British competitors winning a world title both before and after him – Jerome figured that Vic Charles was the epitome of what a karate competitor should be. He was tough, resilient and could execute every technique impeccably. Though I never had a conversation with Vic Charles, I have a feeling that he would return Jerome's compliments because as fighters who had started their competitive careers in the 1970s both men were aware of each other's talents and the sacrifices that were necessary to become world heavyweight champion.

My opponent in the semifinal was tall, fast and wearing a newly acquired England badge. The bout was just how I wanted it: fast and furious and we had slugged it out quite ferociously until the bout had ended as a draw. A 'sudden death' extension was announced: the next to score would be the winner. I was confident, as I had figured out my opponent's tactics and thought I would have won the bout if I'd had just a little more time. He came at me with a fast combination which finished with a kick to my head but with a move that was reminiscent of my fight with Trog in the dojo, I had avoided his punches and stepped inside the kick to deliver the winning score right on the point of his chin. I was in the final, or so I thought for the split-second before my opponent started to roll around the mat clutching his face. Such was the quality of his playacting that I was promptly disqualified. He miraculously recovered but was soundly beaten in the final and I never again got the chance to fight Vic Charles.

As I left the arena with a bronze medal in my hand, several senior instructors from other styles approached me while knowingly shaking their heads and offering me their commiserations. 'Diving' and feigning injury, once the preserve of continental soccer players, had gradually crept into karate and was becoming more prevalent. The great champions, many of whom had competed in the 1970s, when karate bouts were a lot tougher, would never have stooped to such tactics but an increasing number of younger competitors were quite shamelessly doing so and by their actions they devalued what it is to be a karate champion. Perhaps I just did not have the talent to be a really top class competitor but from that day my ambition to be one was severely diminished.

*

As there were changes going on throughout Wado Ryu, so there were changes happening within the YMCA dojo. Throughout my adolescence, the dojo had been an undeviating influence on me. It was not the physical place, as the venue had changed three times during my training; it was something about the mood, ethos and spirit of joint endeavour that had altered subtly. Eddie Cox and Declan Byrne were spending their evenings teaching at several clubs throughout the area and Chester Morrison and Jerome Atkinson were also seen less at the dojo. With Chester it was work that took him away but Jerome had decided that if he were to succeed at international level he was going to have to train quite differently to the rest of us.

Every afternoon, after a long day on a building site, Jerome would meet up with Declan and go through a relentless series of combinations and reflex work on the punch-pads. There had been a few sceptical voices raised in the changing room about this strategy but they had been silenced when in the previous year he had won the European all-styles heavyweight title.

There was also another ambition that kept Jerome away from the dojo: tired of his work as a carpenter, he had decided to go to evening classes so he could attain the necessary qualifications that would enable him to enrol on a teacher-training course. That also attracted mumbled comments of derision but Jerome was more farsighted than most. It took years of hard work but in applying the same sort of drive he had used in his karate, he did go on to become a highly respected teacher in a school that was situated in one of the most deprived areas in the town.

The absence of so many senior grades meant that the only other instructor left to supervise our training during the evening sessions was my cousin Ewart. Training in the dojo under Ewart's direction took on a new emphasis. Combat had always been the primary objective of the black belts' instruction but as Ewart's prospects of competing again at international level had receded, he had looked for places other than the competition arena to show off his fighting prowess.

Following twenty minutes of kick and punch combinations up and down the dojo, the rest of the class were still gasping for breath as I rushed toward Ewart. As instructed, I grabbed the white canvas collar of his gi with one hand and threw a controlled punch with the other. He blocked my technique with an exaggerated movement so all could take note. Pulling me closer, his elbow stopped short of my chin, while he took time to demonstrate the vital striking points. My teeth were clamped shut as I anticipated his next move. His forearm made contact with my jaw and turned my head. Grabbing my hand which gripped his gi, I was twisted and turned before being swept off my feet. Although disorientated as I hit the concrete floor, I still had the awareness to tense my stomach before his stamping kick landed with a thud on my mid-section.

"In a real situation," barked Ewart, his teeth bared, "don't waste time on the stomach. Straight in his balls, throat or face. Have you all got that? On the streets there are no second chances. Once you get them down, you never let them get back up, by themselves."

Everyone present knew that Ewart was talking from experience. "The streets" was a euphemism for nightclub doors, his new arenas. As I was hauled to an upright position to begin the whole process all over again – this time at full speed – I silently cursed him for using me as a thinly-disguised means of polishing the techniques he had no inhibitions about using out on a road during the early hours of the morning. Taking a lead from Jerome, I knew my preparation for the upcoming tournament in Cumbria required a specialized form of speed and reflex drills, with a range of skilled partners, so as to be ready for a variety of opponents, especially the Scots who would journey just a little way south to take on the Sassenachs. But Ewart was busy selecting the same karateka I wanted to practise with to form a group of doormen who would be ready to do his bidding. In a certain environment, the training that Ewart provided would be practical, even life-saving, but as I hit the concrete for a second time I no longer wanted to be a street fighter.

In the ensuing minutes, the sounds of flesh smacking against the hard floor were followed by moans and groans that filled the dojo and forced Ewart to call "*Yame.*" He had reluctantly acknowledged that his own enthusiasm for this particular technique outweighed the human body's ability to absorb such punishment. However, any notion that he was about to make things easier was abruptly dispelled as he began to demonstrate a series of choke holds.

It did not take long for the first student to keel over unconscious. While Ewart worked frantically to revive the green belt who had the misfortune to partner Trog, I exchanged a knowing glance with my partner. The number attending the dojo was almost half of what it used to be and I had a feeling there would be even less at the following session. Although none of us were aware of it at the time, the YMCA karate club was in a slow and terminal decline.

— Chapter Twenty —

Everything can collapse; houses, bodies and enemies collapse.

Miyamoto Musashi — The Fire Book

ANY FEELINGS OF satisfaction brought about by my victory at the Cumbria Open championships had been tempered by the news that Clinton had been readmitted to hospital. As I feared would happen, when his girlfriend had dumped him he had suffered another psychotic episode. Clinton's deterioration had been quite slow at first but to me it seemed that every time he went into a hospital the rate if his decline accelerated and his chances of making a full recovery became even more remote. He was always heavily sedated and unresponsive when I visited him in the psychiatric ward but I when I showed him the impressive trophy I had just won, a smile flickered across his bloated face. "Me and you will be training again soon," he whispered hoarsely.

*

For me, life had largely remained several sequences of routine – but unlike some acquaintances I had known from school and who now languished in prison – at least the nature of the routines was mostly of my own choosing. Three years had gone by since that win in Cumbria and Clinton's hospitalization – and the world had not stood still. While I recognized what had remained constant in my life, I was also acutely aware of the things that had changed.

One of the major changes was that Hilda, Nadine and I had moved from our high-rise flat to a modest semidetached house not far from my parents' home – but not before one last encounter with the gang of skinheads who lived on the top floors. I had come across them individually or in pairs intermittently and nothing more than baleful stares had ever passed between us. As time went on – and I had got myself a better car and another place to live – the bad feelings I had toward them lessened. I figured that Declan Byrne had probably got it right when he had said that I had jumped to all sorts of hasty conclusions about them stealing and burning my old car. Any thoughts of retribution had drifted from my mind – until the night I returned to the flat to check for post a few days after we had removed the furniture. As I went back to my car thoughts of visiting Clinton on the way home meant that I had not taken much notice of the raised voices that came from somewhere beyond my peripheral vision. "Hey! I'm talking to you, you black bastard!" someone shouted.

I finished unlocking the car door before I pivoted around to see four young guys on the other side of the car park. The skinhead I had seen first that day in the lift, shortly after I had moved into the flat, was amongst them. He had allowed his hair to grow a little longer but other than that he had not changed much. He led the other three toward me. At his shoulder was a man who was slightly larger, his pudgy face was contorted with hate. Maybe they had waited this long because somewhere in their befuddled minds they had figured that now I was no longer living in the flat there was less chance of any acts of retaliation from me. The car door was unlocked and I had the option of jumping in and driving away but my running away days were long over. In a move that subconsciously mirrored that of Jerome's when he had confronted with the huge knife man outside the Rising Star, I took two steps forward to meet them. The pair that was at the rear dropped back slightly on seeing this. I knew then they were only going to get involved if they had a chance to kick me while I was on the ground. The two at the front were now up on their toes, bouncing on their heels as they walked. Pudgy-face threw an empty beer can to the ground but all I did was fix my eyes on the guy who now had his arms wide open. He snarled: "C'mon then! C'mon then! C'mon then, you black bastard, c'mon let's have some aggro!" There was obviously a lot of pent-up animosity that had built up within him since our first encounter at the lift. I took another step forward, knowing I would have to take him out in one. I let my arms drop and gave them a small shake to make sure there was no tension in them. Now I could see his lips move and the small droplets of saliva that were ejected from his mouth but I heard no sound. Something strange was happening to me: I felt no fear, no anger but a weird feeling of tranquility had seemed to envelope me. He made his move, in slow-motion I thought, and I was only aware of one of his hands moving as I drove my fist upwards. There was a crack of bone meeting bone as the force of the blow lifted him off his feet. He landed with a thud but I was already pivoting and throwing my other fist into the pudgy face. My knuckles exploded onto the point of his jaw. His reaction to being hit was slightly different: he let out a soft groan as he bent at the knees before flopping flat onto his back. His body shuddered briefly and then went completely still on the tarmac. The other two who were following them stopped in their tracks. Suddenly, they looked younger, smaller and a lot more scared. I was about to tell to them they could walk away if they so wished, until the glint of metal on the ground caught my eye. A knife had spilled from the hand of the first skinhead as he hit the tarmac. I picked it up, before anyone else did, but as I straightened that weird feeling of being at peace instantly evaporated. I became incensed and started to swear at the skinhead who was still lying unconscious. So this bastard was about to try and make my little daughter fatherless. For one microsecond I thought about making a mark on his body or face with the knife so he would always have to live with a reminder of his murderous intentions. Old school friends of mine had done time in prison for stabbing people, one had actually killed a man, and until that moment I had not understood what had impelled any of them to drive a blade over and over again into another human being. But now I knew: the driving force behind their actions had been one of pure and undiluted hate; they had been caught up in a moment in which there been no thought of the consequences. When the moment passed – and the discipline I had acquired from my karate training took over – I held up the knife and said to the two left standing, "When they wake up, tell your mates they were lucky tonight. But if any of you ever pull a knife on me again, I'll leave it somewhere in you. Do you understand?" The pair nodded and I got into my car. It was not until I pulled up outside our new home did I become aware of how much I was sweating and how my hands were shaking. At first, I cursed myself for being so reckless, for allowing pride to prevent me making my escape as the four guys had shouted at me. I looked up to the light in the bedroom window and imagined Hilda and Nadine up there in their new, safer surroundings and how I had risked our futures together because the little boy within me did not have it in him to run away anymore. I sat in the car for another half an hour doing my best to compose myself, before throwing the knife down into a drain and going inside.

The change of location had a dramatic effect on our relationship. Hilda was now a more positive person, a fully qualified nurse, whose newfound optimism had led her to embark on a midwifery course. Both of us had matured in a way that helped us to understand each other's viewpoints a little more. Nadine was now a rambunctious toddler who was attending a local pre-school nursery and in her interactions with other children she had blossomed. As a family, we had grown together.

There were major changes in my work too. 'Arches' closed in 1983 after it had degenerated into the last refuge of every thug in town who had been barred from almost every other establishment. But it was not to be the end of my working on nightclub doors. Fuelled by the desires for furniture for our new home and a newer car, I clambered aboard the capitalist tread wheel like a well-trained hamster and began to work at several clubs. It was during those times that I realized how touchingly naive, and somewhat amateurish, we had been while working at 'Arches'. The world of the professional doorman was a great deal murkier and, as I gradually found out, it was a place inhabited by drug-dealers, steroid-abusers and police informers.

It was the one aspect of my life that troubled my conscience more than any other. In some cases working as a doorman was as nasty and as dangerous a job as one could imagine. The night-club foyer is often inhabited by emotionally stunted men who while not very brave, are capable of extreme violence. During my time on the doors I had seen some unpleasant things – like a man having his face destroyed by a piece of timber until it looked like a mound of raw and bloody steak while four men took turns to jump on him as he lay unconscious, in what the newspapers described as a 'turf war' between two rival gangs of bouncers. Initially, I'd had few qualms but as the violence continued I began to feel that most of it was to do with feeding egos and garnering reputations. My perception about violence and the feelings it once stirred within me had finally begun to change. Where there was once exhilaration was now a slight nauseous pang. Yet although some of it turned my stomach, it was not enough to make me discontinue my work as a doorman. Maybe it should have done. What kept me working in such places was chiefly the money and it helped that I also *felt* one step removed from what was going on around me. I was not like these men, I told myself. But one evening, as I was getting ready to do another stint on a night-club door, I looked down to see my daughter playing with one of her dolls. The sight was so captivating that I sat down. As I watched her play, I wrestled with my conscience and once Nadine was tucked up in bed, I did not bother going out to work. From that moment I had finished with working on nightclub doors.

As for my work at the factory, I repaid the personnel manager's faith in me and passed my Higher National Certificate examination with flying colours. Mr Pearson then had me moved from the maintenance department to the management offices. My promotion did nothing to disguise the racist structure of the management within the plant; as I was the only black person in the offices, my presence somehow only served to highlight it. I wish I could say that I entered my new position feeling like a trail-blazer, or that I was making some sort of statement about equality. In reality, I was an extremely tentative young man whose biggest priority with regard to work was how it would pay my mortgage. Upon his retirement and before he left the factory for one last time, I assured Mr Pearson I had no intention of quitting and I remained grateful to this quietly-spoken man who had profoundly altered the course of my life.

The second departure from the factory prompted me to reap-praise some aspects of human behaviour when Mick Davies told me he was leaving. "No offence," he said, "it's nothing personal, but I really can't work under you." I thought I understood how he felt. I was once his junior and now, nominally at least, I was his senior. To most of my former colleagues in the maintenance department, I was a treacherous 'scab' whose promotion had the ring of thirty pieces of biblical silver about it. I shook Mick's hand and I was sincere when I wished him well. We had shared good times and although we had grown a little distant from one another, what we had experienced was only the normal ebb and flow that is the nature of human relationships.

Similar ebbing and flowing had gone on within the YMCA karate club. There had been growing tensions within the dojo and matters came to a head after Jerome Atkinson won his world title at the end of 1984 in Maastricht. I had taken a special pleasure in his victory when I found out that the man he had beaten in the final was the same one I had lost to in the European under-21 championships. But I also recognized that years of gruelling training had taken their toll on Jerome's body, particularly his knees, and it was only with the aid of two cortisone injections that he had been able to compete that day. When he returned to England, he told Eddie Cox that the world championship final had been his last bout and he was not going to put his health at further risk by competing again. The YMCA had been invited to compete in a tournament the following week but it was not until we were at the venue that our sensei told us that Jerome would not be fighting with us. The air, particularly that which came from my cousin Ewart, became thick with recrimination and acrimony. Eddie Cox's unexpected news had left the team completely demoralized. For the first time in years, we were eliminated in the early rounds and Ewart never fought in a karate tournament again.

From that day, the Wolverhampton YMCA karate club existed in name only. We went through the motions for another two years but we were never again to recapture our glory days. The spirit and camaraderie within the club had gradually vanished. People, times and karate had all changed and although some of the faces remained, many more had left and the end of the fad known as the 'kung fu boom' meant that fewer young men were inclined to enter and put themselves through the rigours of karate training. Those of us who had trained together as youths, were now young men who wore black belts around our waists. Leslie, as usual, seemed to emerge from the chaos within the YMCA unscathed to win three British championships and a European title at lightweight. He was, to any neutral observer, favourite to win a world title in 1986 but an appearance in court led to British karate's governing body imposing a ban which disqualified him from competing at international level. The man who went onto win the world title at Leslie's weight was a competitor whom he had beaten many times and it only served to confirm my belief that the wild side of Leslie's nature robbed him of more things than it had helped him to achieve. And although I continued to do well in competitions, I did not do as well as Leslie, mostly because of a double dislocation of my shoulder which required an operation and a snapped Achilles' tendon. The injuries were very painful signals that my body was neither willing nor able to continue to suffer the severe punishment I had put it through for over a decade. The club had been like a family to me and it was too much to expect that the relationships within the confines of the dojo could continue in the same vein. As my father had said to me as I had left the home in which I had been brought up: two bulls cannot reign within the same pen. Perhaps, then, it was unreasonable to expect that a dozen bulls could remain, never mind reign within the same enclosure.

I continued to see Clinton from time to time and, more often than not, the meetings left me with a heavy heart. He cut a tragic figure, even during the periods when he was free from the worst symptoms of his psychosis. There had been episodes of paranoia but thankfully Clinton was always intercepted in time by friends or relatives to prevent anyone getting hurt and he had ended up being 'sectioned' under the Mental Health Act. With Hilda often by my side, I went to see him in the hospital. Every time I laid eyes on the bloated person who had been consumed by the chemicals that were supposed to alleviate, if not cure, his illness, I could not help but think back to the times when Clinton had the chiselled physique of a finely honed athlete and when there was an energy and sharpness about him. In the years since his illness was first diagnosed, his life had been punctuated with tragedy and incidents that took him back to the psychiatric ward on several occasions and I often wondered if there would be any end to his torment.

I remember, as it approached the end of May 1986, thinking that the following month would mark my twenty-fifth year. A quarter of a century: it seemed a long time to be alive back then. June would be a special month for me and it would also be one in which the members of the Wolverhampton YMCA karate club would come together for one last time.

*

The church was filled with the sombre faces of friends and relatives I was only conscious of for brief periods. The Wolverhampton YMCA karate club and Clinton's friends were present and united in grief, but I sat well away from all of them. Like Clinton had once done, I had closed off myself from the outside world as I asked myself where had *I* been when Clinton had needed me most.

The day before he died, Clinton had called to my house but I had been out, nowhere important. When Hilda had told me of his visit and that he had called around to wish me happy birthday, I said that I would see him during the following weekend. Another time I might have telephoned or tried to find him but I had been left drained on every occasion after I had seen him since his mother's death during the previous year. Clinton had been hospitalized after her death but, with Hilda's help, I had dredged up the will to visit him whenever he had been admitted. We walked the hospital grounds with him and Hilda would sometimes look across as we slowly shuffled along and smiled as if to tell me that *I* was doing fine. It was nearly all too much for me: why had life treated him so cruelly that he had been reduced to this?

With a voice full of well-rehearsed sincerity, the vicar brought my mind back to the funeral service when he asked the congregation to reflect on the ways Clinton had touched our lives. A great wail went up from the back of the church and rippled its way to the front before it reverberated within my chest. My heart felt as though it was swelling and the sensation brought my head toward my knees as I thought my chest was about to tear open and expose the raw pain I had experienced in losing someone I had loved.

There was movement all around me as people got up to file past the open coffin to take one last look. I glimpsed a woman who had a camera in her hand and for a crazy moment I wanted to push her away and shout out that this was not a circus. What were the motives of those who photographed or gazed in at the corpse; a morbid curiosity about what a skilled mortician can do for a body broken by a fall from a thirteenth-storey window, perhaps? As I stood up my head began to spin and I brushed past the woman as I made my way out via a side door.

I sat on one of the low walls in front of the church and while looking across to the tower block from which Clinton had fallen, I tried to imagine his last moments. A hand found my shoulder and I turned to see it was my mother. She asked if I was going to take a last look at Clinton and I told her that I did not want my last memory of him to be one of him lying in a coffin. My mom nodded as if she understood. "Come on then," she said, "they're finished in there now. We still have to put him to rest."

*

More than a month had gone by since the funeral. Hilda had taken Nadine shopping with her and left me to get on with the plumbing job in the bathroom that I had intended to do for almost two years. I appreciated that she left me alone with my thoughts as often as she could.

My mind continually wandered and made my progress with the plumbing so slow that I decided it was time for a tea-break. As I waited for the kettle to boil, I switched on the radio. An old song from the seventies was playing, it was Carl Douglas' hit '*Everybody was Kung Fu Fighting*'. All at once there were images flickering through my mind: of nights out with Clinton, Errol and Leslie at the Colosseum watching kung fu movies; of the time we had been chased by the gang of men and how Clinton had run back to help me; and of that very first training session at the YMCA after he had persuaded me to go with him.

"Clinton, you *were* as fast as lightening," I laughed to myself, in time with the song. At least, I thought I was laughing. It was then I noticed the water on my arm. Confused, I looked up to the ceiling while thinking my plumbing had sprung a leak. I looked to my arm again and saw more water, this time dripping from my nose. Mr. Kovac, my old Hungarian neighbour had been right, not even karate could allow me to win all my battles: I could not fight back the tears anymore. It was at the kitchen table that I wept for what seemed hours as I finally came to terms with never seeing my cousin Clinton again.

Also by Raldon Books

THE CRIME NOVEL OF 2006

Love, Lies and Bleeding

by

J.S. NOON

Former cop Justine Manley is black, beautiful and now a private investigator on the trail of a people trafficker known to police and intelligence agencies around the world as the Falcon. Her search takes her from Toronto to London, where she enlists the help of two debt-collectors named Patrick 'Pinkie' Pinkowski and Roy 'Monster' Haughton.

Justine realizes that she is not the only one looking for the Falcon and his lover. A group of professional killers seem to be one step ahead of her and hell-bent on eradicating anyone connected with the 'Falcon Operation'.

And then there is Roy Haughton's psychopathic brother Glen. He makes his money robbing massage parlours and is planning to take five million from the notorious armed robber Dave Bent. Glen does not know it but he is also sleeping with the Falcon's lover, the enigmatic and very beautiful Sonia, who also happens to be Pinkie's ex-wife.

During her time in London Justine Manley encounters friendship, deception and violence: love, lies and bleeding.

UK	£7.49
Europe	€10.99
Canada	$9.49

ISBN 0-9552169-1-5

For more information on events and forthcoming titles please visit
www.raldonbooks.com